NO TEARS FOR

AIDEN

Chasing an Elusive Dream

BY
VERN HAMIL

Published by Victorious You Press™

Printed in the United States of America
ISBN: 978-1-73406099-4-2

For details email vyp.joantrandall@gmail.com
or visit us at www.victoriousyoupress.com

Prologue

American Airline Flight 1196 landed safely. I was awoken by the clapping of my fellow passengers. As I stepped off the plane, I came to the realization, it was the same old Jamaica, and nothing had changed. Even though I had anticipated seeing some changes in clearing the immigration process in a more expeditious manner. I was disappointed, the lines were long and moving like snails as the Jamaican heat beat down on my skin. Finally, at long last, I was handing over my documents to the Jamaican officers.

"Welcome to Jamaica. What's the purpose of your visit?" the officer asked.

"Business."

"How long will you be staying?"

"Six weeks."

"Enjoy your stay," the officer said as he returned my documents.

"Thank you."

I went outside, a small group of women approached me.

"Any dollars nice lady?" one of them asked

"No," I replied, feeling annoyed. I just didn't want to be bothered.

My ex-husband Clive and his friend Ron were waiting, I greeted them warmly, and then I looked around, my eyes searching, and then I saw her. She was talking to a man in a blue shirt and long black pleated pants. Whatever he was saying to her was making her smile. She then turned her head away and walked toward me. She was a beautiful woman with such charisma and charm. A feeling of mixed emotion from deep within swept over me. She was twenty-six, yet she looked much older. On her face was a look of sadness and resignation. She had been through a lot in her young life, surviving a brutal rape at the hands of someone she trusted, an experience that had haunted her over the years. There was enough blame to go around, but only her rapist was responsible for destroying her innocence. Since then she had suffered secretly and deeply from that incident on the night of her seventeenth birthday.

I walked over to her. "Mandy," I said softly.

When she saw me, she buried her head in my shoulder as I held her in a warm embrace. "I am so sorry, Barbara," she said. "I am so sorry."

"I know. It's not your fault," I tried to reassure her. "He is in a better place now."

I held her and we walked toward her car. "Come on. Let's go home," I whispered.

On the highway from the airport, the cars hurried along the lines of traffic, and my heart was breaking. I had my work cut out for me. The writing was clearly on the wall, and the stars were not aligned in my favor. I had a funeral to take care of, a young mother who might be suicidal to monitor, and a seven-month-old baby who was depending on me for his survival.

Clive drove up the long driveway followed by Ron and Mandy's car. We went inside the house and I was overwhelmed with guilt. Six months ago when I was here, Mandy came home from the hospital, and my son and I had a big welcome-home party for her. I remember him saying, "Mom, this party is for both of us; I will never leave her again." Now Mandy sat beside me on the bed in her room looking frail. For her, I knew we would have to take it one day at a time.

"Mandy, how did it all start?" I asked.

"Barbara, it's a very long story," she said.

"I have all the time to listen. I want to hear it all. How did you two meet?"

She stared at me long and hard and then said, "Are you sure you want to know?"

"Yes," I told her.

Slowly, she began, and for the first time since my arrival, I was afraid of what I was about to hear. It was one of the most heart-rending stories any mother could hear; she was telling this story not only for me, but for all the women who had loved and were afraid to let go. She told the story for mothers who had made the ultimate sacrifice, mothers who had left their children behind, often in unstable homes, in search of a better life in a new country or who were fleeing from other traumatic situations.

Her story is an example of the ultimate price that was paid by both mother and daughter as a result of these sacrifices. I was in for a long night, but I had to know what got us to this point.

Contents

MANDY'S
Story

Chapter One

It was Friday, a market day. The streets were very busy with pedestrians. Motorists waited impatiently for red lights to change to green. The long lines of traffic were bumper to bumper. In the midst of all this was commotion from hagglers and fish vendors selling on the street side. It was hard for anyone to concentrate. The noise and bustle were a nuisance to me, and I had almost lost my balance when he caught me; I was breathing fast as I uttered, "You almost knocked me down."

"I am sorry, Miss," he said with grin on his face as he stopped to pick up my books. I was just seven minutes away from my first period class; I had another three and half blocks to go. "Sorry? You blasted nut! You're sorry, yet you're laughing your head off!"

My temper flared. I snatched my books from him and hurried on my way. Luckily, I made it to class on time. My professor, Mrs. Andrews, was a very stern woman. No one escaped her wrath; any latecomers were always turned away.

It was said that she was a miserable woman, because her husband went back to the United States and forbade her to follow. She always dressed the same, in long skirts or dresses flowing to her ankles. She had long, black hair with flecks of gray. At age fifty-five, she looked fifteen years younger. As I hurried into the classroom and took my seat, she remarked, "Well, Marshall, how lucky you are." I was feeling rather winded and was sweating profusely; and already I was thinking how much I couldn't wait for the class to just be over.

Later, during my lunch break, I discovered that I did not have my identification card. That afternoon, annoyed that I had lost my card, I relayed the encounter I had with the guy on the street that morning to my roommate, Julie Sommers. I could feel a migraine coming on, so we left for home, both of us planning on a quiet weekend ahead of us. The afternoon sky was getting dark and gloomy as the rain clouds gathered, we hurried along the long rows of houses in silence, each caught up in our own thoughts.

Saturdays were usually tiresome for us. After Julie and I had done our household chores and gone grocery shopping for the upcoming week, I was sitting in the living room watching the movie *Intersection*, starring Richard Gere, Sharon Stone, and Lolita Davidovich. I must have watched that movie a thousand times. I did not know at the time, but the irony was that my life would end up mimicking the screenplay of that movie. I was lost in thought when I heard a car pull up in the driveway. My first thought was that it was Julie's boyfriend, Paul Goulbourne, but then I remembered that he had gone to visit his mother in Montego Bay for the weekend. As I moved toward the door to inquire about the car in the driveway, the doorbell rang, startling me. I answered the door cautiously, and I was surprised by the man who stood in the doorway.

"Good evening, Miss Marshall," he began.

"Oh no, not you," I said.

"So you recognize me," he remarked.

"Shouldn't I have reasons to recognize you?"

"May I come in?"

"No," I snapped.

"Is Julie home?"

I stood there with a rather surprised look on my face.

"You know Julie?" I asked, perplexed.

"Yes, she happens to be an old acquaintance of mine."

"Oh—I am sorry. Do come in," I said as I stepped aside to let him in.

I watched him walk toward the living room, his footsteps making tracks on the polished floor.

He was tall and looked more handsome than he had looked the previous day. His skin was dark chocolate, and his hair was well-groomed. He seemed dressed to be going out on a date or something. My eyes were busy sizing him up. He took a seat I did not offer and smiled at me. As I was about to go upstairs to get Julie, he said, "Here, I have something for you."

I followed his hand as he pulled my identification card from his pocket.

"You dropped it yesterday while you were getting your books together. I found it after you left."

"Or did you snatch it from me?" I asked quizzically.

"I think you should thank me," he said.

I took the card from him as Julie walked down the stairs.

"You have a visitor!" I called out to her.

She didn't look surprised to see this unexpected visitor; instead, she greeted him warmly.

"Hello, Michael, nice to see you. How is it going so far?" she said.

"What the hell is going on here? Is this some type of game?" I questioned.

"So you two have already met?" she asked.

"Yes, we have. I just returned the identification card to her. Like I said over the phone, I wanted to make this a surprise, and it was; she almost bit my head off at the door," he remarked.

"Sorry about that. Mandy, meet Michael. He is an old friend of mine," Julie said.

"It's my pleasure, Mister—?"

"The name happens to be Knight, Michael Knight."

"You already know mine, I guess."

"Of course I do, Miss Marshall."

While Julie went to get refreshments, Michael and I struck up a conversation, and before I knew it, and despite our rather awkward introduction earlier, we seemed to be the best of friends. We discovered that we both liked the same type of music and that we both shared a passion for horseracing and even visited the racetracks on a regular basis. However, I was afraid to ask if he was a compulsive gambler. Julie joined us when the conversation turned to politics—one of my favorite topics. Soon thereafter, Michael left, as he said he had a prior engagement. We assumed he was going out on a date because he kept looking at his watch.

After he left, Julie asked me what I thought of him, and I told her I thought he was cool. It was then that she told me that he liked me and that his bumping into me the other day was done on purpose.

Even though I liked him too, I didn't disclose that fact to her.

That Sunday morning, getting out of bed was hard; my headache was gone, but I felt very drained. Julie and I went to church for praise and worship service. The visiting pastor, Reverend Ezekiel Thomas, was tall and skinny and wore glasses on the tip of his nose. He delivered his message to the congregation with a strong voice; the theme was, "God works in mysterious ways." After the service, I went home, and Julie went to visit the sick at the hospital with some of the other church sisters. Later that afternoon, Michael called and invited us to an Oliver Samuels play, which was supposed to be held at the high school auditorium that evening. Julie said no and I got cold feet, so I declined the invitation as well.

It was a long evening with nothing to do, so we decided to go for a walk at the nearby park. It was a lovely Sunday evening as fate would have it. The sky had cleared up, and the sun had returned to brighten up the evening. At the park Julie and I sat and watched children playing and lovers strolling. It seemed people were returning from the play, which I later learned had been very good.

The park had lost its appeal by the time we left; there was a slight drizzle and the sky had darkened. On our way home, we ran into Michael, who offered to accompany us home. As we continue walking, Paul, Julie's boyfriend, drove up beside us. Michael seemed relieved when I didn't go with Julie and Paul, and as we walked together along the long stretch of paved sidewalk, Michael told me about his job and the love he had for his family. He told me he was very close to his family, and it was clear that he had strong family values. I couldn't contribute much to the conversation, or maybe it was that I wasn't ready to talk about my broken family; it was hard enough to deal with, much less talk about with a stranger. Just then, Julie and Paul drove up beside us and asked if I would like to go see a movie with them. I quickly accepted the offer and bid Michael good-bye, taking their invitation as an opportunity to escape talking about the whole family issue.

"We could have invited Michael," Julie remarked as we drove away.

"Have you seen him much lately?" Paul asked.

"No, but I think he is interested in Mandy," Julie replied.

"Is he, Mandy?" Paul asked, turning to me.

"I don't know. I'm really not interested in anyone," I told him.

"You aren't interested in men? What are you afraid of? They don't bite," he said.

"But they sting like snakes," I replied.

"Only if you let them," Julie told me.

"I think you should date generally, and someone will come along," Paul said.

"Let's just close the subject," I stated.

"I'm sorry if I offended you, little sister," Paul said. "I didn't want to say anything, but I wish you would just act like a grown-up and accept dates from men. How long are you going to live such a dull life?"

Paul's words rang true; however, I felt that my life was just fine as it was—no major complications, my heart running free. I was also able to give advice to the love-lorn, criticize Julie and Paul's relationship, and see all that was wrong in everyone else's affairs. Yet, I was hiding my true feelings regarding affairs of the heart; I knew I needed someone—someone who would be more than just a friend. However, I wasn't sure I was ready for dating, deep down I had emotional wounds which left me with ugly scars ---and I couldn't get away from that fact.

Chapter Two

The following evening, I went to visit an old friend, Marie Cross. She lived in a small town ten miles from ours. Marie had suffered a broken shoulder in an automobile accident three weeks ago and was home recuperating. Her daughter, eight-year-old Yori, opened the door with a big smile.

We hugged as I walked into the house listening to her sad tale of school and how horrible her day had been. I assured her that school would get better, but she just gave me that "whatever" look.

Later, after leaving Marie's house, I decided to meet up with Michael, and we went to a small bar where he was scheduled to meet some friends from his old school. The night was cold, lovely, and still as we walked down the street after leaving the Bar. Our time together seemed magical. It was like we had been down the same road before in a past life. Here we were together like no two people ever were, and all the fear in me just melted away.

It seemed so incredible that a man who had just entered my life could capture my whole being so quickly, but it happened. The profound effect his presence had on me was somewhat troubling, though. I had never felt this way before, and I knew I needed to enjoy every moment of it. It seemed like we were a part of something—something no one knew about except us.

When we reached the front of my house, Michael stopped and held my hands so gently in his as he looked into my eyes. It was at that moment I realized that what we had together was the beginning of something I had never yet dreamt of, something I had never hoped for until now. He squeezed my hands and said, "I'll see you tomorrow, Mandy." We wished each other good night and he left.

I entered the house and went up to my room. I wondered what was really happening to me; his promise of seeing me the next day sent chills up my spine. I looked at the clock on the wall; it was almost midnight, and I already wished it was seven the next morning.

In bed that night, my heart was beating fast, and I could not sleep as I was waiting—yes, waiting—for dawn to break. I finally dozed off at about two thirty, and when I awoke, it was six thirty... I got up and got dressed and made my breakfast of bacon, eggs, toast, and coffee. I gathered my things and then left, and at the bus stop, Michael was there. We waited for the bus together and agreed to have lunch that day.

The restaurant where we dined for lunch was very romantic; the walls were painted and decorated in pastel shade of blue with fruit designs, making the atmosphere feel bright and warm. The dim lighting came from the two candles placed on each table. At the windows the beaded bamboo curtains hung daintily and swayed in a gentle breeze. At the far end there stood a bar with the drinking glasses hanging from the ceiling. The patrons seem to be enjoying "Happy Hour." A delicious scent came from the kitchen and filled the entire place. When our waiter arrived, we ordered curried lobster—my favorite—along with a tossed salad and fruit juice, and it wasn't long before our food arrived. The food, the tempting aroma from the kitchen, and the intimate setting of the tables were enough for anyone to see that this was a five-star restaurant. It was the first time I was out with Michael in such a warm atmosphere, and his company really impressed me. I noticed by his table manners that he was raised well, and I could also tell that he wasn't trying to put on a show for me. After dinner Michael asked to stop by my house later that night, but I regretfully had to decline. I had assignments to complete for my next class.

Later that afternoon I was sitting in the living room reminiscing about my romantic lunch with Michael when Julie walked in. She said she was tired; I guessed that she had had a bad day. I wanted so much to tell her about my lunch with Michael. Michael occupied all my thoughts, it seemed. I realized I needed to talk to someone about it, and the only person I had to share my feelings with was Julie. As she came out of the bathroom, she looked at me.

"Wake up. You seem to be dreaming."

"No, I was just thinking," I said.

"Thinking about your exams?" she asked.

"Not really, but I wanted to talk to you about last night."

"Last night? What about last night?" she asked.

"It's Michael I want to talk to you about."

"Michael? What about him? Don't tell me you are letting Michael capture your thoughts."

I paused. She was right, but somehow I just didn't want to admit it. My pride wouldn't let me do it after that awful experience I had been through when I was seventeen. I told myself I had no use for men. I didn't hate them, but I would keep them at a distance. So how could I tell Julie that I had feelings for Michael?

I braced myself for her response to what I was about to tell her. Would she dismiss the whole thing as a crush, or would she be happy for me that at long last I was ready to face the world again? As I waited for her to get dressed so that we could leave for class, I wondered what she would say.

As we walked the three blocks from the bus stop to our classes, I bravely asked, "Julie, what do you think of Michael?"

"Oh, he is very nice and charming; I can see why you would be drawn to him. But he is a player."

"So one minute your boyfriend is telling me to date him, and the next you are saying I should run from him?"

"No, that's not what I am saying," she said. "You are the one asking for my opinion, and I am telling you with all honesty, and you are getting defensive."

"I am not defensive; I just want to know why you think your longtime friend is no good for me."

"Did you find out if he was involved with anyone?" Julie asked.

"Well, he's not married."

"I'm not talking about marriage here, Mandy. Did you ask him if he has a girlfriend?"

"No, I didn't, and to be frank, I really don't care; every woman should fight her own battle when it comes to love or affairs of the heart."

"You are a selfish little bitch," Julie snapped at me.

"Yeah, after what my mother went through, do you think I would be sorry for any other woman?" I asked her pointedly.

She crossed the street and continued to walk away from me; at that moment I thought to myself that I could beat myself up for asking her about Michael.

As the weeks passed, I saw more of Michael, and whenever he traveled for work, he called me and we would talk for hours.

Since Julie knew Michael, I hoped to get some background information on him. But after our last conversation, whenever I mentioned his name, she just stared at me, and I was disappointed. So I went to the source: Michael. He confirmed that he had had a girlfriend but that the relationship was over. I thought everything through once, twice, and then I even prayed about it. Our relationship just felt right. Michael had told me he was the proud father of two children but had no intention of rekindling a relationship with their mother. He also clearly stated that he was not yet ready for marriage. For me that was just fine; all I wanted was someone who would make me feel like a woman, someone who would love me unconditionally, someone I could trust, and someone I could confide in. That was all I was asking for at that moment, not marriage.

I recalled his words to me one day as he held my hands. "Don't be afraid, Mandy."

"Michael, I'm not afraid. I just don't want to get hurt," I told him firmly.

"I'll never hurt you, Mandy. Remember that, I'll never hurt you," he said once again even more convincingly.

I looked sadly into his eyes as he continued.

"You will have to trust me, and with time I will prove myself," he said.

Despite his promises, it took me weeks to make up my mind about continuing a relationship with Michael.

Something was holding me back, and I was fighting to rid myself of old demons. Finally I gave in, and I told Michael that I was willing to be in a relationship and I was willing to let him prove that he was different from the man who had raped me on my seventeenth birthday and had left me with his child. When I found out that I was pregnant, Dr. Jones had strongly recommended that I terminate the pregnancy. The months following that abortion were a living nightmare, and even now the fear was very much alive again.

I could clearly remember the words Dr. Jones had said to me as he took my hands from my face wet with tears.

"Mandy, you are pretty young, but you have to be strong; you have to fight back the memories and forget."

But how I could forget, I had thought.

It was my seventeenth birthday, and my dad had held a party in my honor. He had invited the entire town. The party got under way at 9:30 p.m., and Dad and I opened the floor for dancing. At ten, the dance floor was crowed. The music was blasting away, and everyone was excited. I was having a wonderful time. At 3:00 a.m. the crowds began to drift away, and I went to my room to change into something more comfortable. A few minutes later, there was a knock on my door.

"Come in," I called out.

The door opened and Jim stood there.

"The girls are ready," he said.

"Where is Mom? She is supposed to see that they get home safely."

"Your mother was passed out on the back porch, and your dad took her to her room," he said.

"Poor Mom. She had too much to drink again," I said, fighting back my anger. She was only there for my party and she had to embarrass me; she had promised she wasn't going to drink that night.

"Are you the only driver available? Where is Marcus?"

"He went home early," Jim said. "He wasn't feeling well."

"OK, I will be down in a minute," I replied.

Slowly, Jim closed the door and walked away. I wished that I didn't have to accompany Jim; however, I went along. After taking the girls home, Jim and I sat in the car discussing the party. Then, suddenly, he drew me close to him and forced his lips on mine. I immediately pulled away.

"Come on, Mandy. What's wrong? You are a big girl now," he stated.

"Please take me home," I said.

"Sure," he stated.

He started the car, and we drove on in silence. I sat gazing through the open window. I almost jumped out of my seat when I felt his hand on my shoulder.

"Why are you so nervous?" he asked.

My heart sank as he turned off the main road onto a back street and stopped the car. The next thing I knew, he was pulling off my clothes, and I start screaming, "Let me go! Stop! Stop!"

My cries were useless, however, as I laid there helpless.

"We are going to make love," he said softly into my ear.

I could smell the liquor on his breath as he rubbed his face against mine.

"No! No, stop," I cried.

The pain was unbearable and he wasn't going to stop.

Then I heard his mocking laughter, and then nothing.

When I woke up, I was in my own room.

I didn't remember how I got there from the car, I tried to get off the bed, but then I felt the pain, and it all came back to me. I buried my head in my pillow and let my tears flow freely. *How could I let this happen to me*, I thought.

Jim was one of my father's hired help. I knew if I told my father what had happened, Jim would be dead and my father would spend the rest of his life in jail. I had already lost my mother to another country, and I was not prepared to lose my father to jail; he was all I had. Furthermore, I didn't want anyone to know that Jim had raped me. I was torn up and crushed inside knowing that I had to keep this secret for the sake of us both. For the first time in my life, I actually missed my mother, even though I didn't even go to the airport to see her off. I cried all day and the next, and the next, I couldn't control myself. I eventually told my father that Jim had made a pass at me and that I was uncomfortable with him around, so he was fired.

After that traumatic experience and its aftermath, I had stayed away from men, until now. Michael now stirred in me what no one else had, even though I had nothing to compare the feeling to. I knew I was falling for him faster than the countdown to midnight on New Year's Eve.

Michael had invited me over; he was going out of town on a job assignment and didn't really know how long he would be away. Sometimes he would be gone only a few days, and other times he could be gone for months; it all depended on how long it took him to complete a specific assignment. As I stood over him, watching him pack his clothes, he looked at me and said, "I hate to leave you. I hope you understand."

"Don't worry, babe, I know you have to work," I assured him.

"It will be very hard without you; my life has completely changed since I met you."

"Please, Michael, don't talk that way; you are making me sad. I am going to miss you too."

He walked over and put his arms around me; his lips were soon against mine, kissing me softly. Before I really knew what was going on, my body responded to his touch. As he kept kissing me, he then slowly removed my clothes and led me to his bed. I lay on the bed as he placed little butterflies kisses all over my body. He cupped my breasts in his hands as his mouth sought my nipples, sucking from one to the other. My brain went into shutdown mode. I could see and feel his hard erection pressing against my body as he continued to kiss me. Then I felt his tongue in my ear as he inserted his fingers into my vagina. I started calling his name; my body was longing to be fucked in a good way, so I begged him to take me to the land where people say milk and honey flows. I had the milk and needed his honey.

"Oh, Michael, oh, Mike," I cried as he put his dick inside me. I wanted to scream from the pain, then slowly, as I lay there panting, my body began to move with his. He placed his mouth over mine, and he tasted sweet, but what he was doing to me was heavenly divine, and I didn't want him to stop. Then, like a lightning bolt, I was having my first orgasm, tears rolling down my cheeks as I held onto him and screamed out his name.

We lay there as I slowly came back to earth. As he held me in his arms, I started to rub my hands over his dick in small strokes. He looked me in my eyes, watery with tears, as I pleaded to him for more. We made love passionately.

Suddenly, there was a knock at the door. We ignored it at first, but then the knocking grew louder, and I finally had to admit that someone out there was intruding on our privacy after such blissful moments.

"Who is it?" Michael called from inside.

"It's Sandra. May I come in? I need to talk to you for a minute."

Michael looked at me then at the closed door.

"Yes, Michael. It could be something with the kids," I said as I got dressed.

Michael opened the door, and Sandra stood there dressed in a denim skirt and a white shirt. Her feet neatly fit into the slippers she wore, and her hair was pinned up.

If she was surprised to see me, she didn't say so. But I could see the hurt in her eyes as her tears gathered.

"Hi, Sandra. It's nice that you are here," I said.

"Is it?" she asked scornfully as she stepped inside.

"Yes, Sandra, it is," I stated.

Her eyes moved to the unmade bed then to Michael, who was wearing only his briefs.

"Seeing is believing. Now I see you have someone else and I'm not welcome anymore," she said to Michael. "I'm sorry if I interrupted anything, but I didn't know that you had company."

"I'm sorry, Sandra," Michael stated flatly.

"Sorry that you used me? Is that what you are sorry about, Michael?" she asked.

Michael didn't answer.

"I think I'd better leave," she said.

"No, Sandra. Wait a minute," I said. "I think I better leave so the two of you can talk."

"Don't go, Mandy. There is nothing to talk about," Michael said.

"On second thought, I am not leaving until we discuss what I came to talk to you about, so you can ask your lover to wait in the next room until I am through," Sandra said defensively.

I took the book *Hotel* by Arthur Hailey and walked into the next room. I couldn't hear what they were saying from where I was, but I knew a heated argument was going on.

Then I heard Sandra screaming. I dropped the book and rushed to the room. Michael was standing against the wall, and Sandra stood over him with a knife in her hand.

"No!" I cried. "No, Sandra!"

"I am going to kill you! I am going to kill you!"

"Sandra!" I rushed towards her.

"Don't touch me! Go away!" she shouted at me.

She then slowly dropped the knife to the floor and began sobbing, which then turned to long wails of crying. Michael was petrified.

"I didn't know she had that knife," Michael said to me.

"I hate you, I hate you!" Sandra yelled out.

And with that she left. I watched from the door as she hailed a cab. Then I turned and looked at Michael as I walked away,

Chapter Three

The following day I went for an early morning walk to ease my mind of the tensions that had been building up inside of me. Paul had invited Sandra over last evening, according to Julie she called crying on the phone .and he wanted to comfort her.When I returned home, Paul had left for work and Julie was in the kitchen preparing breakfast. I smelled the strong Blue Mountain coffee as she poured some from the teapot.

"Where have you been?"

"I went for a walk."

"That's very unusual for you. Did you have a good night's sleep?"

"No, I couldn't sleep, actually, and then in the early hours of this morning I had a very weird dream, Julie. I think I need to move," I said firmly.

She turned and looked directly in my eyes.

"What are you talking about?" she asked.

"Julie, I will be moving. Please don't try and talk me out of it."

"But where will you go, Mandy?"

"I could go back home and get a roommate, or I could share Jean's apartment."

Jean was my rich friend. She had everything she ever wanted, except for being able to put on a few pounds. She was born prematurely at seven months, and during the time we were growing up, she was very skinny and had remained that way. She was incredibly beautiful with long, flowing hair to her shoulders. She had a good sense of humor and could make anyone feel better about a bad situation.

"Mandy, would you really go back to Kingston to live in that house?"

"Why not? Dad has moved out, and the house belongs to me. Mom might object to me staying there on my own, but Dad could care less."

"Mandy, you think living with the Joneses along with Jean would be the best thing for you?"

"I really don't know, but I do know moving is better for me right now," I told her.

"I'm sorry about what happened yesterday between you and Sandra. I know Paul's been making some stupid jokes about the whole thing, but he is your brother, and men will be men."

"Excuse me. I know you didn't just say that!" I said as I felt the anger welling up inside of me. "He is nothing to me—nothing! We live in the same house. How could he even think of inviting *her* over? How insensitive could he be?"

"Paul and Sandra grew up together; he is only trying to help her."

"No they didn't. They ran around as kids for their first ten years," I corrected her.

"Whatever you might think of the situation, though, they were always close."

"I understand," I said, although I was far from understanding.

"Mandy, you don't have to be upset. But Paul isn't going to stop Sandra from coming over."

I looked at her. I could hardly believe her last statement, and then I said, "I know either you or Paul sent Sandra over there yesterday knowing I was there."

"Why would Paul do that?" Julie questioned.

"Then it was you!" I pointed my index finger at her accusingly.

As she turned around to face me, I could see the pain in her eyes, and the look on her face confirmed my suspicions.

Paul was supposed to be my half brother, and even though my mother never accepted him as family, my father did everything to give him a good education. He was sent off to London to attend a prestigious boarding school, and whenever he came home for the holidays, my mom and I would go on vacation, leaving him to spend time with our dad. So my mother started putting a wedge between us at an early stage. Looking back now, I can see how my mom suffered all those years with the shame of my father's infidelity. It wasn't just the fact that Paul was born outside the marriage; my mom struggled because of the reputation of Paul's mother. That situation turned my mother from a respected high school principal into an alcoholic; she refused to go for treatment and ended up losing her job and most of her high-class friends.

The Roots Club lay in the center of town, and go-go dancing was just being introduced. Amy, Paul's mother, and Dotty, Sandra's mom, were best friends who danced there together. The Roots Club was my father's favorite watering hole. It was rumored all along that my dad was having an affair with Amy. He and my mom never moved in the same circles, so she was the last to know about his affair and the child; however, when she found out, she told my dad she wanted a divorce. Yet it never happened, and seven years later I was born. Paul shared his mother's last name, but everyone knew he was my dad's child, and because of that my mother could not stand the sight of him.

After several years of living the nightmare of hearing my parents' frequent fights, I had deluded myself to accept this as normal. I told my mom I didn't want to sleep in the room next to the master bedroom anymore, so a new room was decorated for me. I picked new furniture and bedding, and I thought I was in Heaven. I thought I wouldn't have to listen to them arguing anymore in the middle of the night, listening to conversations a child has no business hearing. But my escape was short-lived, as my mom began coming to my room and crawling into bed with me, stroking my hair as she sobbed uncontrollably. My father would come home late, as usual, and my mom would stay up drinking, and then the fights began. One night was particularly frightening. She came into my room and got into bed with me and began stroking my hair, and I just laid there pretending to be sleeping. Then she vomited all over me—in my hair, on my face, and all over my pretty pink pajamas. Then she dragged me down the hall like a rag doll, turned the shower on, and let the water just beat on my skin. My dad heard me hollering and came to find us; he bathed me and tucked me into bed in one of the guest rooms while he changed my bedding. I didn't see my mother for two days after that, and I didn't care. I was coming to hate her more with each passing day.

I was startled as the phone rang, bringing me back to the present, Julie answered;

"It's for you" she said as she walked away.

"Hello."

"Hi, Mandy."

"Michael, I am so glad you called."

"What happened? You sound under the weather."

"Michael, I am moving tomorrow"

"Moving? Why?" he asked.

"I will tell you about it later."

"Where are you moving to?"

"I have made arrangements to stay with Jean, maybe, for a short while until after my final exams."

"How does Julie feel about all this?" he asked.

"Julie? Well, we have talked about it, and she understands."

"Are you sure you are doing the right thing?"

"Well, I have no choice."

"OK, we will talk later; I will come and see you tomorrow sometime in the evening."

"But Michael, I'll be fine. There is no reason for you to come all this way," I said.

"I am coming no matter what you say. I miss you, Mandy. I miss you more than you will ever know."

"I miss you too, Michael."

I hung up the phone and start packing my clothes. There was a knock on the door.

"May I come in?" asked Julie.

"Yes."

The door opened and she walked in.

"You are really going through with this," she said as she looked around my room. There were clothes scattered on the floor, including a pile of those I intended to give to charity, and there were empty drawers open. Clothes hangers and belts, along with my suitcases, were on the bed.

"Yes, it isn't all that hard," I told her.

"Your brother is very upset about you leaving."

"My brother has yet to say so to me," I pointed out, smiling.

"I am so sorry, Mandy," she said. As she moved to embrace me, I stepped back.

"We moved here together, Julie, because we were best friends. When you told me Paul wanted to come to live with you, I didn't object, even though he and I don't get along. I tried to make it work for all of us. That was more than my own mother did for me." I paused for a moment. "But let me ask you this. Why do you do anything your lover-boy ask of you? You should be on my side, not his and Sandra's!"

"I know, but I didn't know you and Michael were actually sleeping together. It was a mistake. You were right before. I did tell Sandra you went to see him."

"Why did you do that? It was none of your business, Julie," I screamed at her.

"I know, but Paul said you should date men, not sleep with Michael," she said with a smirk.

"I pity you, Julie. It's all about Paul. You don't have to convey his message for him. He can tell me himself."

"What, so you can tell him about his whoring mother and how much you hate him? Just let it go, Mandy. Let your anger go," she pleaded with me.

I hung my head in my hands, trying to think. Then I quickly looked up at her and shouted, "Get the fuck out!"

Chapter Four

The next morning, I didn't see Julie, while I was busy getting my things in order. I went looking for her. She was sitting on the back porch talking to her mother on the phone. She looked up and saw me standing in the doorway and abruptly disconnects the call.

"Hi," I said.

"Hi," she replied coldly.

"I am sorry about yesterday," I stated.

"No, save it Mandy, you are not sorry, you know that, and I know that."

"Would you like some lunch? I am starving."

She smiled at me, then said, "That would be nice."

We sat in the kitchen eating tuna sandwiches and drinking iced tea. I remember how many mornings we sat at this same counter drinking coffee and flipping through the morning papers, and a small tear gather at the corner of my left eye. I quickly composed myself. We spend the rest of the afternoon making light conversations. We wanted or rather I wanted to part on good terms. In spite of everything; I didn't want to be ungrateful. There were times when Julie was the rock on which I leaned on for moral support through my many battles with emotional pain caused from my parents. Nothing can change that.

It was almost 3:00 p.m. when Jean arrived; we quickly put my things in the car while the movers loaded my bedroom furniture on their truck. I hugged Julie and took one last look at the house that had been my home for four years. Sandra was coming up the driveway as Jean and I were getting ready to drive away. Being the nice person that she was, Jean stopped to say hello.

"Well, it's been a long time since I last saw you," Sandra said to Jean.

"I'm very well and doing fine," remarked Jean.

"Put on any weight?" Sandra asked.

"Still trying," Jean said.

Sandra stares at me with her big brown eyes, and I stared right back at her. She waved to Jean as we drove off.

After we arrived at Jean's and unpacked my things, I sat on the balcony and began to tell Jean about the events that led me to make the decision to move. She too agreed that my living situation had become a hostile one.

After Jean and I shared a nice first dinner together as roommates, Paul and Julie came over unexpectedly.

"Mandy, I want to have a talk with you," Paul said and asked if he and Julie could come in.

I knew it before he even began. As always, Julie had told him about our little heated conversation. "You accused me of making you unhappy and blamed me for making you move."

"Paul, now is not the time for this," I said.

"I am very sorry about you leaving; all I was trying to do was help Sandra. She is a nice girl, we grew up together, and she has two kids. Michael really hurt her; he didn't even tell her it was over. He just stopped going by her house."

"Are you saying they were still sleeping together?" I asked, trying to remain calm.

"Yes, Mandy. He lied to you. They didn't break it off as he made you believe. Michael is not the type to settle down with one woman."

"Why didn't you tell me this before?" I asked, now visibly upset. "Why didn't you tell me he was connected to Sandra?"

"I didn't want to get into your business."

"But you are my brother; you should have told me. It would have made a difference."

"I'm sorry, Mandy, but I saw how happy you were when you were with him, and I didn't want to spoil that happiness."

I looked at Paul, his head bowed, his eyes not meeting mine, and in spite of our sibling rivalry, I knew he was telling the truth; my head began to hurt.

"Why did Michael have to lie? Why?" I asked myself. Paul came over to me and put his arms around me.

"I'm sorry, Mandy," he said.

Julie was out on the balcony with Jean having a drink, and Paul and I went to join them.

I felt the first sting of regret in having started a relationship with Michael.

Later, Julie and Paul were ready to leave, and Jean and I walked them to their car. I watched as their car drove away, and for the first time that evening, I wished that I was going back home with them. I stayed on the balcony for a while; alone, just gazing out at the mountain in the distance, thinking that was my young life before my eyes—a mountain.

I went to bed that night feeling sorry for myself and feeling more alone than ever before.

The following evening, Michael arrived, as promised. I introduced him to Jean as she looked him over. She was impressed by his personality. Michael had a way of being loved by everyone; it just happened naturally. He thanked Jean for letting me stay with her, and Jean told him that it was something she had hoped would happen for a long time ago. Michael was planning to stay the night, and I was not going to mention the conversation I had had with Paul the previous night. I was going to wait and see if he were a liar by nature or just lying so he could have both of each worlds. However, after avoiding his eyes all night practically, it didn't take him long to ask what was upsetting me once we were alone in my room.

"Is there something wrong?"

"No. Why?" I asked.

"I feel like you are acting cold toward me," he said, pulling me closer.

"Everything is just fine," I assured him and tried to assure myself.

"Let's make love then," he said playfully as he started to peel off my nightshirt, his hands then travelling down to my panties.

"Yeah, let's make love," I said, giggling. Even though I knew we shouldn't, I just couldn't resist him.

That night, despite any qualms I had about our relationship, I slept peacefully. The next morning, Michael left early. I enjoyed being in the house with Jean, and I was quite happy. Even though I had put what Paul told me out of my mind, I kept wondering why Michael had lied to me before, and to think that Julie had supported his story was unbelievable.

***

Soon it was summer, and my dad had invited Jean and me to spend a week with him in Spanish Town.

We were happy about the idea, and I discussed it with Michael. He too was happy about my dad's invitation. My father had never invited me before because he thought I resented him for what had happened between my mother and him.

We left Monday morning by rail. Traveling by rail was safer than driving. When we arrived at the Spanish Town Railway Station, Michael was there to meet us. I was really surprised when I got off the train and saw him standing there. He greeted me with a kiss and hugged Jean warmly. He was so happy, and we talked about what a wonderful time we planned to have. Michael officially lived there now; he was promoted on his job and with the promotion came added responsibilities. Therefore, that will be his home for the next few months. While we were waiting for Dad to pick us up, Michael had to leave for a meeting, so he promised to take us on a tour of a well-known house one day during the week we were there.

Dad arrived at the station shortly after, and we left.

The car drove up to a house on Fairfield Close and stopped. The house was similar to the one I'd grown up in in Kingston, and the memories came rushing back. My little sister ran toward us; she was only four and was unfortunately the final straw that had led to my parents' divorce. She was cute and beautiful, and I could see that my dad adored her. Behind her I saw my stepmother, Michelle, affectionately called, "Shelly," standing in the doorway.

I found myself for the first time not feeling any resentment toward Michelle. We hugged each other warmly. I caught Jean giving her the evil eye, but I quickly took control of the situation by complimenting Shelly on her lovely dress. We all had lunch together and made small talk at the table. Later that evening, my dad took Jean and me to a movie. No sooner than we got home, Michael came over, and I introduced him to my father and to Shelly, who I introduced as my dad's "friend." The three of them chatted for a while before Jean and I had a chance to talk with him. It ended up being almost midnight when he left.

The next morning my dad called me to his office. I sat down, crossing my legs and dangling my six-inch heels. He got straight to the point.

"What do you know about Michael's past, Mandy?"

The question caught me off guard as I watch my dad exhale from his pipe.

"What past?" I asked, feeling blindsided.

"Well, his father was an alcoholic, worked with the Alcan Bauxite Company for many years. Everyone loved him and respected him when he was sober—" I began feeling a burning sensation in my belly; I knew what he was going to say was not going to be good. My father cleared his throat as he continued. "But he was a mess when he was wasted. One night while at work, he was crushed by one of the rail cars. Michael was the eldest son, and he was always with his father, but luckily that night Michael was asleep in one of the sleeping quarters instead. It took the crew a couple hours to locate the body under the railcar. But Michael saw it all once he woke up.

He was obviously traumatized and did not speak for weeks."

"Oh my God!" I started crying.

"I know, Mandy. But I just wanted to tell you because I thought you should know," he said as he inhaled his pipe once more.

After finding out the shocking news of Michael's past, I was feeling numb inside, but it was only our second day and I felt it was important to keep our plans of going to tour the town.

The beauty of the town was unique; the old broken buildings had been replaced by modern structures. History had recorded Spanish Town as the first capital of Jamaica; it was later changed to Kingston.

We visited the Arawak Museum. Later that afternoon, my little sister, Allei, wanted to go to the park, so Shelly, Jean, and I took her there. It was surprising to see how she took to me.

She looked so innocent, so young and gentle. I could tell she was going to be a beautiful woman.

The day was well spent. Allei, Shelly, Jean, and I all had fun, and we also did some shopping. That night my dad took us out to dinner. Sitting there together in the restaurant enjoying each other's company, I thought about how this was the family I had craved growing up.

But that part of my life was irreplaceable, and as a young woman I had learned to pave my own way and had been doing so for as long as I could remember.

After breakfast the next morning, Michael picked Jean and me up and took us to his place.

The outside garden was lovely, and the scent of flowers filled the air. He had a very large flat with a living room, dining room, and large bedroom. The floor was carpeted wall to wall, and the furniture was new. It didn't have the look or feel like a bachelor's pad, though, and I couldn't shake the feeling that the apartment had the touch of a woman. This was yet another red flag that I chose to ignore, however.

We made ourselves at home and sat down to have a drink while being entertained by good, solid music. The stereo played "Cover Me," a cut from a Percy Sledge album. The music must have gotten to Jean as she quickly excused herself and left for the mall. Michael seized the opportunity to get close to me. I wanted to move away, but I couldn't. He led me to the bedroom. We laid there in each other's arms as the last selection on the album started playing "You're All Around Me." We both realized how true that statement was for both of us. The music stopped, and his hands moved to caress my body. In the distance somewhere I heard "Imagination" playing. I listened to the words; they were so very real, I thought, as I fell asleep in Michael's arms.

It was about 4:00 p.m. when Michael and I left to go back to my dad's house. Michael and I, along with Jean, my dad, and Shelly, spent the rest of the evening playing indoor games. I felt very uncomfortable with Michael being around my dad after what I had learned about his past. Thank God he left after the second game. The rest of us watched a late-night movie on television and then retired to bed. All this time I was thinking of my alcoholic mother and Michael's father; luckily my mother had escaped her demons by running away, yet Michael's father died with his. So this was the inner connection that was pulling us together like two lost souls. I wondered about his restlessness and how he seemed to use sex to drown out his pain, yet I was responding to his optimum desire. I thought of all the nightmares he had after losing his father under such tragic circumstances, and I could relate through my own nightmares dealing with my mother. A bond had been forged between us, and we each found what we sought in the other—a place to bury our pain and find common ground.

The rest of our week in Spanish Town passed by quickly, and soon it was time for us to leave for home. Michael drove Jean and me to the train station. Slowly, the train pulled into the station, and as Michael held me in his arms, God knows I didn't want to leave, not when Michael was there, but I had to, and so I stood beside the waiting train and kissed him good-bye.

I boarded the train with tears in my eyes, knowing I was leaving Michael behind.

Chapter Five

The town hall was crowded, and the lights flickered on and off as the contestants for the beauty pageant were about to make their first appearance. I was there to cheer for my old schoolmate Marcia Wallace; she was favored to win. The master of ceremonies moved forward to the microphone.

The room suddenly became quiet as all eyes were now fixed on the stage.

At that moment I found myself thinking of Michael. It had been six months since I had last seen him. He was completing a training course in Quebec, Canada, and we had only communicated by telephone.

Each time he called, he would ask, "Mandy, are you OK?"

After not seeing your lover for almost six months, how OK can a young woman be?

I questioned myself.

"Ladies and gentlemen, your attention please," the emcee began.

I stared at the empty stage as the emcee continued.

"The contestants will first appear in their formal dresses."

I watched as the ten contestants came on stage for the first time. They were greeted with loud applause. It was an enjoyable evening, and it was no surprise when Marcia Wallace walked away with the crown and a check from the National Commercial Bank.

The pageant was over, and having no idea what the night held, I left feeling entertained. Upon reaching my gate, I heard a familiar voice call my name. I stood there frozen, not knowing if I should turn and run away or run to the arms that were waiting to welcome me.

Michael was standing there with a wicked smile on his face. I rushed to him, and he held me in his arms, kissing me wildly. Tears of joy ran down my cheeks as we walked toward my car.

At home we had a long talk; we had so much to talk about, and he said he had completed his training and would not be going back to Quebec. My head was spinning, and I was acting like a typical schoolgirl in love. It had been a long time since we had been together like this. I held him so close that night, I wanted this to be forever and when morning came, he wouldn't let me go, and with all the passions wrapped up in my soul like a Christmas present I gave him my all.

The following evening we went to see the movie *Smile Orange*. Tensions in the audience were running high as one of characters made love to a hitchhiker he had picked up along a country road. We could hear nervous laughter coming from the men. I could tell they were getting excited; even Michael squeezed my hand as the couple reached their climax. It seemed as if all the men were in heat watching the scene.

After leaving the movie, we went to a nightclub and danced the night away. I wasn't much of a dancer, but I was willing to learn, even if it meant I had to embarrass myself a few times on the dance floor. Looking back now, I wasn't even doing it for me; I was doing it for Michael.

Shortly thereafter, my dad had a long talk with me late one night, as he thought I was getting "out of control."

I was spending a lot of money on stupid things, liking buying a new bedroom set when I didn't really need one, going on shopping sprees, and going to the racetrack with Michael. Sometimes I would go to the racetrack with Jean, and then Michael would be right there. Sometimes things would get really ugly, him wanting to leave with me and me wanting to leave with my friends. My thing was that if we didn't go together, then we shouldn't leave together. My dad heard about these little disagreements, and maybe more than he was willing to say. He told me, "Mandy, Michael is bad news. I am warning you. He never got therapy after his father died, so he still has a lot going on."

I thought to myself that I never got therapy after my rape either because I was so ashamed and because of the bad blood between Paul and me I couldn't confide in him, and as time passed, I never confided to anyone about what had happened to me.

"Who are you to tell me anything about relationships?" I wanted to say. "Mom would say the same about you." But instead, I thanked my dad for his concern and reassured him that I could take care of myself. However, deep down, I was furious. *How dare he?* Then I slowly remembered Paul's words: "Michael is not the type to settle with one woman." A smile came across my face, though, as I reassured myself that that was then and this is now; he only has one woman now. I wouldn't stand for his philandering ass, so he better get it right; if I am the one, then I am going to be the *only* one.

In mid-June, I saw Sandra at the supermarket, and at first I was surprised to see her in these parts. I thought maybe she was here visiting friends. I made a beeline for the next aisle, but she had already seen me.

"It's 3:00 p.m. Do you know where your man is?" she asked.

I just looked at her and walked away. Actually, I felt sorry for her. Little did I know then that I was the one to be pitied.

Later that evening, Jean came home very upset, but whatever it was, she didn't want to talk about it. However, I later learned that she too had had an encounter with Sandra earlier that day and that Sandra had said she was on her way to Montego Bay to spend the weekend with Michael.

That statement left me breathless. Michael was indeed in Montego Bay on a job contract.

I quickly dismissed the unpleasantness from my thoughts, though, but deep down I knew that it was true.

A few days later, Michael came back from his joyous weekend, and I had made up my mind to quit.

So when he came over for a visit, I sat there and listened to his explanation. How does one explain spending a weekend with an ex-girlfriend? I could see the guilt written all over his face as he tried to explain his way out. For the first time, I realized that my dad was right; this man was indeed bad news. I was hurt beyond words, but instead of calling it quits, I told him I just needed my space.

I was really thinking of dating other people. There was this cute guy Bobby who had a crush on me, and he and Paul worked together, so sometimes Paul would invite me to lunch when they were going. There was no spark between us, however. I also didn't really know if my brother was trying to get me away from Michael because he and I were blood and he cared about my well-being or because he wanted Michael to be with Sandra for their kids' sake. So I had a talk with Paul and I asked him outright if he had known about Michael's past and his relationship with his father prior to his father's death. He told me yes and added, "I don't think he is capable of loving anyone or being in a committed relationship. Use this time to break free from him and don't look back."

I wanted to heed Paul's advice, but I missed Michael so much. To get my mind off of things, I started volunteering at the local hospital, I went to church every Sunday, and I stopped going to the racetrack and to nightclubs. I was waiting in the wings.

Four months later, Michael asked to come stay the weekend. We thought we would give the relationship another chance. Being apart had made us both miserable and needy for each other; however, what should have been a very promising weekend turned out to be a very trying one. I was like a puppet on a string. I just couldn't resist him even though the memories of the past kept coming back to me. Michael was a good lover. The sex was great, and when we made love, we became one. We just couldn't get enough of each other, and I didn't want to give all of that up yet, so prior to our weekend together, I sent him a letter instead.

Dear Michael,

I knew from the start that this relationship depended on both of us to make it work. You cannot want to be with me and continue sleeping with your ex.

Every woman at some stage of her life wants to know that she is loved by someone and, more importantly, that she is loved by the man she loves.

And that goes for me as well. Every woman knows that sometimes all she needs is the air that she breathes and his love. I am not forgetting that others have the same feelings but fail to express them like I do.

Have you ever taken the time to question your feelings for me—your real feelings?

I wish you weren't so unrealistic.
Mandy

Two days later his reply came:

My Dear Mandy,

It was with a heavy heart that I read your letter. To be honest, I must say that I have hurt you more than once in the past. I have lied to you, and now you find it hard to trust me, but you still love me, for which I am glad.

I love you, Mandy, and you know it; no matter what happens between us, I will always love you.

You are a woman who has no fear in expressing herself. Very few women could have written me that letter. I am assuring you that I need you and that this relationship will go on. Please do not compare yourself to others. Remember you can only be you, and I love you. All I am asking is for your forgiveness and that you keep on giving me the strength to go on. We will have a lasting relationship.

Love you,

Michael

I read that letter over and over, but Michael's words felt empty, and they did not ease my mind.

I knew he was coming for the weekend, and I could hardly wait to tell him in person how I was feeling deep inside.

That Friday afternoon I sat in the living room and listened to Jean as she repeated a conversation she had had earlier with Sandra, but the most shocking news came when she told me Julie had been over to see me. Paul had walked out on her and had left town with the bank manager's daughter, Kandi Rogers.

Kandi was a little spoiled brat who was still in high school. She lived a privileged life, and her father gave her everything. At seventeen she had a BMW convertible with tinted windows.

She was drop-dead gorgeous, and she knew this and played it to her advantage. Paul should have been staying away from her, but instead he seemed to be captivated by her.

He had told me once that he was going to make a life with her, but I brushed it off thinking he had to be joking. He had been with Julie for years and had put her through so much by forcing her to have an abortion when she wanted to have their baby. Now there was this. But Julie was always the instigator for starting trouble between Paul and me. She knew we couldn't stand each other because of how we had been groomed to be, and she used that fact to her advantage every chance she got.

"How is Julie dealing with this?" I asked Jean.

"Sandra called a short while ago and said Julie is taking it very badly and that she has locked herself in her room and refuses to talk to anyone."

"Has Paul been in touch with anyone?"

"No, that was what Julie came here to find out. She wanted to know if he had called you."

"Why would she think that?"

I knew Paul would call me soon; we had put our differences aside and had become really close.

Paul and Julie were not happy together, even though she did everything to please him.

I picked up the phone and dialed Julie's number. It rang for about two minutes before someone answered; it was Sandra. I asked to speak to Julie and waited.

"Mandy, he is gone; he even took most of his clothes."

"He will be back," I said.

"Do you know who he's with now?"

"I heard from Jean, but don't upset yourself so much over this; you knew all along that he was seeing her. You even complained to her father," I said.

"Are you on his side? You should be on my side!"

"Julie, someone once said, 'you can't run from the truth; it will run after you, pass you, and stand in your way, where you will have to face it then.'"

She started sobbing on the other end of the line.

"Did Mr. Rogers call?" I asked.

"Yes, he called earlier, and he was very upset."

"He should be. Kandi should be concentrating on her schoolwork, and Paul should know better."

"What if Paul doesn't come back?"

"He will be back, and you know it; I will be over to see you shortly."

Even though I was trying to reassure her, I wasn't too sure this time. Paul was no angel, and she knew it.

I hung up the phone and walked to the kitchen to get myself a Coke. A car was coming up the driveway, and Jean stood by the window as the car approached. It was Mr. Rogers's car.

The car stopped and we held our breaths as the man who got out of the car was not Mr. Rogers but Paul. Jean looked at me as he slammed the car door and walked toward us.

We sat in the living room, and Paul told us his side. It was bad news for Julie. He wasn't going back to her; Kandi was pregnant, and he planned to marry her within the next two weeks.

"Are you sure this is really what you want?" I asked him.

"Yes, Mandy. I love her, and I have to make this right."

"What about Julie? How could you do this to her?"

"Things happen. I need you to come with me over there, though."

"There, where? That's your home; I do not want to be a part of this."

"You are a part of this, and I need your help," he said pleadingly.

I thought after all the things we had been through over the years that it was only fair that I support Paul and Julie equally. To be honest, Julie was my friend, but I felt no pity for her, especially not after she had bad-mouthed my relationship with Michael. So the evil witch or the bitch in me told me to go see her pain. I looked at Paul, trying to figure out how Julie was going to take this final blow.

Paul was the man she loved and adored; he was the man she couldn't live without. How would she take losing him to someone else?

"OK, Paul. I will go with you under one condition."

"What's that?" he asked.

"That you don't go over there and give her hope of reconciliation."

"Mandy, I am going to tell her like it is. Let's go," he said.

The drive to Julie's house took less than fifteen minutes. We got out of the car and walked toward the door. Paul let himself in and led the way to the bedroom. Julie lay there crying, and Paul stood in the doorway for a moment with a placid look on his face, and then he walked over to the bed and sat down beside her. She looked at him with tears running down her cheeks.

"Paul, you can't tell her now," I cautioned.

"Tell me what—tell me that he is in love with her and wants to be with her?" she said, her face wet with tears and her eyes swollen.

I looked to Paul, and he moved forward, closed the door, and told her everything about his relationship with Kandi.

It was then that I realized that things don't always work out the way we want them to. Michael was in my life and I would rather live in his world than live without him in mine. Michael had given me so much strength, so much courage, to live my life again that I hated to break things off with him. I finally felt like I was living because I had a man—a man I loved, a man who had changed my life, a man I didn't want to leave. I wanted to hold onto him; I wanted to share a lasting love. But, given the strains of our relationship, would I ever be able to make my dreams come true?

That remained to be seen.

Chapter Six

It was New Year's Day. The sun shone brightly as the flowers in the garden swayed their heads to and fro. The holiday spirit was certainly in the air as people very merrily wished each other love, prosperity, and a long life. However, this day would be with Julie forever. Jean had gone to get her hair done for the occasion that afternoon. I sat in the living room crying my eyes out. I tried to control my emotions. I knew Julie would be over any time, and I didn't want her to see me crying; it would only make her feel sorry for herself.

I opened the door as I heard a car coming up the driveway. I went outside to meet Julie. Sandra was helping her out of the car. Julie forced a smile as she saw me, and I gave her a big hug. She was very pale as she followed me inside.

"Are you all right?" I asked her.

"Yes," she whispered softly. I watched her closely as she held on to the side of the car for support.

"Are you really attending the wedding?"

"Yes, Mandy. I want to stop that wedding more than anything else."

"Julie, I don't think that is a good idea. Nothing you say will stop Rev. Miller from carrying out the ceremony."

"I know, but…"

"But you will only make a fool of yourself."

"Mandy, you're right. I'll have the whole church laughing at me. I won't be able to take the humiliation. But Paul said he is trapped into marrying her because she is pregnant," she stated.

"I think that might be a good reason, but there is a lot more to it," I added.

"What are you talking about?"

"Well, they are society people, and that's what they do. They don't have kids out of wedlock, and secondly, Paul is smitten with her."

"Society my ass. We could say the same about you. People like you and Kandi who have rich fathers who cater to your needs will always show some form of entitlement."

I looked at her and shook my head, and then I headed for the door.

***

The big, beautiful Baptist church stood on a hill overlooking the city. It was known for its capacity to accommodate large gatherings, and this occasion was certainly one of them. Kandi was in her last year of high school while Paul was the senior vice president of her father's bank.

They were 'society people,' as I called them, even though Jean's opinion seemed to differ. Paul might have been trapped by getting Kandi pregnant, but he had really fallen in love with her; the pregnancy had simply pushed marriage to the forefront.

Kandi's father had owned and managed the savings and loan bank in town for over forty years, and when Kandi's mother died in childbirth, the entire town rallied around Mr. Rogers, giving him comforting words, and baby Kandi had given him the will to go on. The town folks had treated Kandi like a princess from an early age.

The whole town seemed to have turned out for the wedding. People were on the outside looking in through the open windows to witness the marriage of Kandi Rogers and Paul Goulbourne.

News reporters were all over the building. The organist started playing "Here Comes the Bride." I looked at Paul standing there awaiting his bride; he was so handsome.

I wished it didn't have to happen like this. I watched Kandi and her father walk toward Paul, who was now smiling. Kandi wore a white off-the-shoulder dress with a long train. She looked stunning.

I listened as the congregation sang "Blessed Be The Tie That Binds."

The music of the organ rang out melodious, and the sound of these words echoed outside throughout the streets.

Blessed be the tie that binds
Our hearts in Christian love;
The fellowship of kindred minds
Is like to that above

We share our mutual woes
Our mutual burdens bear;
And often for each other flows
The sympathizing tear.

In the front row everyone was smiling as the couple took their vows. Paul gently placed the ring on Kandi's finger. The crowd outside was orderly. The congregation rose to sing the hymn, "O Perfect Love." A wave of fear came over me as the hymn began.

Mr. Rogers smiled broadly, which caught most of the church's attention. Somehow my mind flashed back to Julie in the apartment. At that moment I had told Jean that I was leaving and excused myself and went outside to my car. My mind was blank as I drove home, only to see that Michael was there when I arrived.

Immediately, Julie rushed over and held me close as she sobbed uncontrollably.

"Is it over?" she asked.

"Yes, it's all over," I told her.

She held me close, and we cried together. I cried for her as well as for myself. All I could think was what if Michael ended up doing the same thing to me? How could I let Julie cry alone?

I looked at Michael as I consoled Julie and as he looked away, I told myself I wasn't going to be no man's fool. We sat on the Porch without saying much to each other. Later that night Michael and I went to a nightclub. We were entertained by good, solid music. We sat there talking, trying to discover what we had lost along the way.

It was midnight when we left. The night was cool, and we might have had a little too much to drink. Thank God we weren't driving. As we stumbled along the road trying to find our way home, Michael was getting more and more difficult. At one point he was even sitting in the street; looking back now, it seems very funny that he was so wasted that night.

I finally got him home, and he went to sleep on the floor instead of the bed. I took a shower and crawled into bed.

I woke up the next morning with a terrible headache. Michael had somehow found his way to the couch and was stretched out like a log. Jean entered from the kitchen and was laughing hysterically. I was a little embarrassed at Michael's behavior the previous night.

However, Jean said it was no big deal. Men get a little loose at times, she had said. I still felt really stupid over the drunken incident and Michael's behavior. That evening we all sat down to dinner, but everyone was still talking about the previous afternoon wedding, which had mixed reactions.

After dinner Michael and I went for a walk by the park. We spent the night together. After we made beautiful love, I heard him say, "Heaven help us."

The next day I sat in my dad's office and told him everything that was going on between Michael and me. My dad was not pleased; he said it wasn't enough and that he wanted to see me get married.

He also said that the relationship was not going to work and that he thought I should break it off. He said it was a waste of time to think that Michael was going to change his lifestyle. My father was totally against our relationship.

The following week Michael was presented with an award for his outstanding work.

I went to the presentation, then left to celebrate, yet it was too good to be true. We went to the Moonlight Club, where we were later joined by his coworkers and friends.

We had a superb time. It was a night that I will always remember because even now I can't escape the memories. I can remember his tender touch that set my whole being on fire, his warm kisses, and the way he held me in his arms as we made love passionately.

In retrospect, I think it was the sex that was keeping us together; I just couldn't get enough of him. Whenever we made love, he took me places I had never dreamed of. I don't know why I loved the sex so much; it might have been that I used it to erase my horrible rape experience, or maybe it was just a natural thing between us.

A week later Michael was working in my neighborhood, and I was looking forward to a happy week being near him; however, it didn't turn out that way.

Monday evening I took a bath and then sat down to dinner. I spent almost an hour at the table all by myself. It was 9:00 p.m. and Michael still had not arrived, even though I knew he had been off duty since six. *What was keeping him?* I asked myself as I got dressed and walked to the apartment that had been given to him by his company. From outside I could see he had a visitor. The person turned toward the light, and I saw that it was none other than Sandra.

I turned and walked away. On my way home, I thought I was going to faint.

I tried to sleep that night, but I couldn't; the thought of them together was enough to make me have nightmares. I cried and cried, and sleep eluded me. It was midnight, and I still had six more hours to go, which passed by so slowly. I reached for my pen and writing pad and wrote the following letter:

Michael,

This should be no surprise as I just couldn't refrain from writing you.

I am faced with the question "Are you so important that two women should be waiting to be in your company?" I waited up for you last night while you were with someone else.

You are very selfish, and you don't care about my feelings; you are not concerned about hurting me.

You take me for a woman whom you can take for granted, a woman whom you pity.

A woman whom you feel sorry for and whom, out of pity, you shared a little time with.

I, in turn, took you for a man—a man who could give his love without pretending.

A man who could care enough not to hurt my feelings.

I thought your past way of life was a closed chapter, but last night I realized that the fucking roles of past years were about to play out another episode in my life.

Let me tell you something: enough is enough!

I need a man…

I need a man who will love and care about me.

I need a man who will be committed.

I need a man who will honestly love me.

Am I asking for too much?

There is always something about you that will remain a part of me, and for that I will always remember you.

Mandy

After delivering the letter, I didn't see Michael for the rest of that week. I heard he left on Friday.

The following Sunday evening I had an unexpected visitor, my pastor. I then confessed the whole story to him, and he asked me to break off my relationship with Michael and return to the fellowship of the church. I thought I had made up my mind to leave him for good this time, however, I told my Pastor, I loved Michael too much to leave him. He explained to me that such a relationship would only end up causing me more heartache and pain.

I listened to him as he pleaded with me to break it off. I just couldn't, though, and then he asked, "Mandy, do you love man more than God?"

"No, Pastor," I replied.

He then rephrased the question. "Mandy, do you love God more than this man?"

I did not reply.

"Mandy, I am so sad to know that I was the one who baptized you in God's holy name, and now you have let the devil take hold of you; the only thing I can do for you now is pray for you."

I listened as he bowed his head in prayer:

"Eternal God I come to You this night in the name of thy only Son Jesus Christ. I come to you with this dear sister's problem. Oh God, she is confused. Help her to realize that when man fails, you will lift her up.

"When man has put her to shame, you will not see her suffer because you are a God of compassion. Help her, dear God, to see the light before it is too late. Soften her heart; help her to turn from her wrong ways, because she knows what she is doing is not right in your sight. These mercies I ask in your name. Amen.

"May God help you," he said.

I watched him as he walked to his car and drove off. I ran to my room.

The Bible was the first thing in sight. I opened it, and this verse met my eyes: "But fornication, and all uncleanness, or covetousness, let it not be once named among you, as saints…"

I took my eyes off that verse, but then I looked further down and there was another that said, "Let no man deceive you with vain words: for because of these things cometh the wrath of God upon the children of disobedience."

I tried to reason those verses away. I closed the Bible and tried to concentrate, but I was more confused than ever. Then there was a knock on my door and Jean walked in.

"Are you fighting back the will of God?" she asked.

"No, but going back to the church now is not the answer," I said.

"You better think it over and go back before it's too late," she warned.

"Do you think something bad will happen to me?"

"I don't know, but God always gives us time to prepare for him before he lets us feel his punishment," she said.

"How could God punish me seeing I don't have the courage to leave Michael?" I asked.

"Maybe it's because you take Michael for a possession that you cherish and don't want to give up, but you might very well lose him," she stated.

"No, I won't. He will always come back to me."

"Yes, Mandy, he will come back to you when he sees that you can't live without him, and at that time he won't come back out of love but out of pity," she said.

"Jean, please leave me alone. I really want to sleep. Good night."

"Good night, Mandy" she said.

She left the room, and I closed the door. That night I tried to sleep, but something weighed heavily on my mind. I took up the phone and dialed Michael's number; the phone rang without an answer.

The next morning I saw Jean watering the plants in the garden, and I called her to my room.

"Did you sleep well last night?" she asked.

"I couldn't sleep at all," I told her.

"Did you pray about your problem?"

"I tried," I said.

"You don't think God can change your mind about loving Michael?"

"Yes, but I don't want to stop loving him."

With that, she walked away, and for the first time in my life, I felt like running away from it all.

In my quest to find love, this journey was about to take me to the dark side of hell. I was confused, lonely, and hurt. But I was out to get Michael; no matter the cost, I wanted him to be mine.

Chapter Seven

The building on the left of the number seventy bus stop at Papine turned out to be the College of Arts, Sciences, and Technology. I walked slowly toward the registration block. There were some two hundred students waiting to be registered for summer courses, which were offered by the college in conjunction with the Ministry of Education. After the registration period, the students were told to assemble in Ferguson Hall, where we were addressed by the supervisors of the courses. It was noon when the students left with strict orders to report for classes at 8:00 a.m. the following morning.

That night I called Michael and told him the relationship was over. He was very upset and blamed my dad for my decision. However, he said this would be a trial period and that as soon as my studies were over, he would sit and talk over the whole thing with me. But my mind was made up. After a thirty-minute conversation, I hung up the phone.

During that week I pretended everything was all right, but it wasn't long before Mark Francis, one of the fellow students who sat beside me, suspected all was not well. While at lunch one day, he took the opportunity to interfere.

"You are not enjoying lunch these days," he remarked.

"Not really," I replied.

"Seems you have something on your mind that you need to get off," he said.

"Mark, there is nothing to worry about," I replied.

"Don't lie to me, Mandy. I have been watching you for days, and the only reason I have kept silent until now is that whatever is bothering you is not affecting your assignments, which is good, but you are not eating, and as soon as you get a free minute, you bury yourself in a book; it is as if you are blocking something from your mind."

I looked at him from across the table.

"All right, Mark. I have something on my mind, something I want to forget, but I might as well tell you because I know you won't give me any peace until I do."

"Take it easy, Mandy. I'm only trying to help. Don't be so guarded."

I picked up my drinking glass, and Mark looked at me with searching eyes. If only he could have found the answer without my telling him; then maybe he would have forgotten the whole thing. I put down the glass, and my eyes met his.

"Mandy, are you all right?" he asked.

"I think so," I replied.

"Why is whatever it is so difficult to talk about?"

"It is not difficult, but private," I said.

"OK, you don't have to talk about it. We can close the subject. It's just that I hate to see you looking so sad," he said.

"I broke up with my boyfriend." I sighed, a frown on my face.

How I got the words out I don't know, but somehow it came freely.

"Broken relationships—are you serious?"

"Yes, Mark, it's the truth. Michael and I have decided that it's over."

"There must be something more to it; tell me everything."

I stared at him for a long time, and then I started to tell him what really took place. We were so caught up in our conversation that when I finished telling him all that had happened and looked around, I noticed that the lunchroom was empty and the cleaners were busy taking up the dishes. I gazed at my watch; it was 2:30 p.m.

"Are you going back to class?" I asked Mark.

"No, I'll get your things and see you home," he said.

"Thanks."

I watched him walk toward the classroom door; Mark seemed to be so understanding that I couldn't help thinking about the happy husband he would be for a perfect wife. We walked to the bus stop and waited together in silence.

Later that evening I called Paul. He was happy about the birth of his son and Kandi's good health. For the past year, he had been happily married and was enjoying his new job as a radio personality. We talked for about twenty minutes, and then he said, "Mandy, I have a feeling something is wrong."

"No, Paul, everything is OK," I reassured him.

"How is your love life?" he asked, the sound of concern in his voice.

"Same as usual," I told him.

"But you deserve much better, Mandy," he remarked.

Lord knows I need help, I realized I couldn't help myself I felt like telling him everything, but I changed my mind.

"I know, Paul, but after I complete this course, I have some sorting out to do," I said.

"Well, Mandy, take care and remember I am always here if you need me."

"Thanks, Paul. Bye."

I was so conflicted with my conviction. One day mine and Michael's relationship was over, and the next it was the same as usual; it just depended on who was asking.

That night I sat thinking about Michael—thinking how living only for his love made me feel so happy. I felt like life wasn't worth living when he wasn't around. I liked to think of him, dream of him, talk of him, and love only him. At that moment there was a feeling of longing—yes, I longed to be in his strong arms and feel his warm, sweet lips on mine. To feel his fiery, magnetic body against mine—oh how I loved his body! I desperately hoped he felt the same way.

I hoped he would miss me, long for me, remember me, and wish for me when I wasn't near him.

Like the song said, "I wish you never happy with anybody but me." That was my wish for him.

My mother always said, "Be very careful what you wish for because you might just have it." It was very selfish of me then, but I used to think how stupid—what would be the point of wishing for something you really don't want? Had I known then what I know now, I never would have quoted those words. I felt like all that I had lived for was lost. I would never be able to love and trust anyone as I had done with Michael. I told myself I would get over it, but there would be scars and plenty of them. I then realized that love or men weren't important to me anymore. All I had ever wanted, loved, and worked for was gone. Michael had been everything to me; I had wanted it all. And my all was Michael.

The phone rang; I answered but got no response from the other end. I sat there watching the leaves sway through the open window, and it was there I realized that maybe I should really walk away and try to love again with someone else; however, that was all wishful thinking.

Two weeks later, the course I was taking was over, and Michael came over to talk for a while, which turned into almost a whole night, and then I gave in. Michael was back in my life. I hoped for the last time things would work out. While my head and everyone close to me were telling me -to move on, I keep reflecting on my own parents. I always felt that my mom could have worked it out with my father for my sake. I blamed my mother for not being stronger and not being able to withstand the ups and down of a marriage. I did not see the pain my dad's infidelity must have caused her, and instead, I had grown to hate her, especially in her fight to get sober. She had had many relapses; it was only now I saw that she was fighting so hard in order to get custody of me. The divorce was really nasty, and everything was brought up, and both the emotional and financial aspects of their lives were put on display for everyone to see. The final blow to my mom was when I told the court I wanted to live with my father. Paul had advised me against making that decision, telling me then what has now come full circle—that I would basically be on my own with no guidance. But I argued that yes, I could handle it; I had been raising myself for a long time—nothing changed. However, there were times when I really missed my mom. She would have made sure I got the counseling I needed after I was raped. Instead, I carried my cold shame for all these years under a blanket. Was this why I was hanging on to Michael? Maybe it wasn't too late and I could still get some help. I promised myself I was going to see Paul and talk to him about it.

The next three months were filled with Christmas festivities, and we planned to host a Christmas party. Everyone was having a good time, but no sooner than the party was breaking up, Sandra was at it again. She called Michael out on the balcony and engaged him in an hour-long conversation. My problem was that I was too blind to see that a relationship between Michael and me could not survive under such conditions.

Chapter Eight

It was another new year, and during the beginning of the year, people made their resolutions. In previous years I had made them but had been unable to live up to them; however, this time I made just one. It should have been quite clear to Michael what I was pointing out to him. We had a long conversation on the phone, and he told me that he understood and that he knew I wasn't asking too much. He promised to give up Sandra. And he did—only to take on Jenny a few weeks after.......

Jennifer Muir was only fifteen years old when she dropped out of high school due to her first pregnancy. She had that child and was now attending a business college where she was pursuing accounting and other related business courses. She and Michael had met one rainy afternoon three months ago at a party given by her brother to mark his second wedding anniversary. However, it wasn't until Valentine's Day when I noticed the card she sent him that I first became suspicious of their relationship.

That weekend I went to visit my dad, and Michael was working in the area and was on the night shift. It turned out to be a very unpleasant situation; he couldn't even find time for me, and when I left that Sunday, he wasn't there to say good-bye. On my way home, I had made a decision that if Michael was losing interest and didn't want me in his life that I would never talk to another man; instead, I would go back to the church. But was the church the answer? Something was terribly wrong with me being with this man, but all I could see was that I loved him. Was it because I wasn't raised in a loving home, making me eager for affection, that I misunderstood emotional abuse for what I was seeking?

When my dad moved into his new home with Shelly, I should have stayed with them. Instead, I went away to college; I didn't want to be near them. Shelly was just a few years older than me, and I wasn't going to listen to her. I saw her more like a big sister, but we never got that close. My dad had put his wild ways aside, but I could still hear the bickering and fighting of earlier times in my heads. That picture has never left me, so when I sought solace in being alone, that was the only time I felt at peace.

The following week Michael was with me, after dissing me the week before, but I put that aside. I just went along with the program, acting as if it never happened, and we enjoyed each other to the fullest. Soon it was Friday, and he had to leave again, but I had a surprise for him. It was a portrait of love that I had dedicated to him:

Love to me is You

Love to me is more than just a feeling in the spring

Or the warm and loving feeling the thought of you can bring.

It's more than just the loneliness I feel when you are not around.

But just the presence of your lovely and thoughtful care resounds.

Whatever and whenever betides…

Remember love to me is you.

I know I love you more each day,

And I know that's a love I wish would never stray.

All across the ocean, over the mountains and below the plains,

Birds will sing and a melodious voice will ring out as if to say…

You are a part of me…

Yes, you are a part of me, and now and always…

Love to me is you.

To a woman love is life…

To me life is you…

I wish you were with me all the time, my love,

Just to see the reflection of love in your eyes;

to hold you in my arms and feel the magnetic power of your body…

Transmitting its power to enforce me in your world of ecstasy…

Endlessly there is no doubt that love to me is you.

That afternoon I presented it to him. He held me in his arms for a long time; he didn't leave that night.

"Mandy, do you really mean every word you wrote?"

"Yes, Michael, I do."

"Are you sure?"

"Yes, Michael, I am sure. I love you so much."

He held me in his arms and kissed me softly.

"I love you, Mandy. Sometimes you might find it hard to believe, but until the day I die, I will love you still."

He sealed that remark with a kiss. I watched him move toward the living room while I listened to the sounds of Percy Sledge singing "You're All Around Me" blazing away in the room. He continued to kiss me as the record went on. His lips sought mine while he stripped me of my clothing.

As he placed tiny tingling kisses over my body, I shivered all over, and I softly whispered his name. He was now lying on top of me, and we were making love; I moved my body gracefully to keep up with the rhythm of the music. As our bodies clung together as one, sheen of sweat spread over my body. We rolled over in each other's arms, as the record went on playing that soothing song. Making love with Michael was the closest thing to heaven I could imagine, and I reached out to him and he kissed me. I fell asleep in his arms, and the next morning when it was time for him to leave, he still wouldn't let me go. Here was where I felt wanted, and I could attest to the fact that my gorgeous boyfriend was the best lover in the world; I didn't have anything to compare him to. I was so tempted to go out and find another man, to see how soothing making love with someone else would make me feel, but I couldn't. I kept remembering my first time and how rough and horrible that experience was, from the ripping off my clothes to the forcedness of someone's body on mine to the painful penetration I had endured that night. Thinking of those things always made me think twice about going with someone other than Michael.

Three months had passed when things began turning for the worse again. That weekend when I went to look for Michael I found Sandra at his apartment. I said to myself, "Lord, not this time. I am not in the mood to argue with her over Michael." She looked up and saw me standing there in the doorway. I really wanted to give her a good ass-whooping, but my dad would have been too embarrassed, so I just walked away. I kept my hurts to myself, and for the next couple days my migraine was on a daily schedule.

The following week when I saw Michael, we had a big, unpleasant argument, like so many we had had before on the subject of him keeping his tool in his pants, but no, he always had to be using it. That Wednesday night I paid him an unwelcome visit with one intention.

It was 8:15 p.m. I walked to the door and entered. He lay there reading the book *Detained* by Parnell Charles. He kept on turning the pages while I gazed at him. At 1:00 a.m. he was still reading, and it was almost two when he finally stopped. His eyes were burning, and he was tired. His eyes were watery, and he wanted to sleep, but I wouldn't let him—not before he made love to me. I was going to be "the great seducer" tonight, and I would not be denied. I couldn't hold back my tears any longer. I began to sob loudly. Here was a man I had devoted my time to—a man I loved. My heart was beating fast; one could hear the sound of my beating heart echoing with the wind. I needed him so much, and he was keeping me waiting. He looked at me long and hard, then he wiped the tears from my eyes and kissed me. I felt his hands caressing my body, and I knew he wasn't going to stop. He embraced me in his arms, cupping my breasts as he entered me; he was kissing me wildly and adoring me as I moved my body gracefully under his. Soon he held me tightly in his arms, and I heard him remark, "Who could ever say no?" So he made love to me. I was that good that he couldn't refuse me. I already knew that, but what I didn't know was how desperate I was for someone to love me that I would put my pride aside.

Even though he had my heart, he was just playing me. The sex felt empty this time; it wasn't rough sex, but something was missing. I thought to myself that I ought to leave him alone and find myself a good man; maybe it wasn't too late to call up Glen and apologize. He was a decent man, and he was the first man I ever kissed, and right up to that fateful day when I met Michael, Glen was the man for me. He was now a police officer, and my mind reflected on those wonderful love letters we had exchanged while he was at training school. We had lived in the same part of town, and he had his eye on me and had the decency to ask my dad permission to date me. On our first date, we went to an event at the local cricket club. In his arms I felt so safe and secure, and when he kissed me, my heart just melted. I knew he loved me, and I had fallen for him also. My dad and Paul liked him, so what could have gone so wrong? Me meeting Michael. I will forever regret not pursuing the relationship with Glen I was too embarrassed to crawl back to him and ask for his forgiveness, though. Anyone playing with a full deck would have done just that, but not me—I still wanted Michael.

Chapter Nine

I was really getting tired of everything in my life. My mother had filed for me to come and live with her in the United States. I came to spend four months with my mom and decided I wasn't going to stay. I was glad I had had that time with her. She shared some deeply personal things with me, and it was then, for the first time, that I saw the hell my father had put her through. She was afraid for me that I would end up like her, even though I was not drinking. My mother had encouraged me to reach out to Glen; she told me to go and talk to him and tell him how sorry I was about our relationship and ask him if he was willing to give it another shot. What I didn't tell my mom was that Glen had moved on. So I came back to right where I was four months prior.

My relationship with Michael was indeed breaking down, and it was four months after that seductive event that I saw him again. Each time he came left me with visible scars; however, I couldn't face the immense loneliness I felt when he wasn't around, my heart ache for him all the time. God knows why he returned time after time. This time he was back again, and like the song, "those funny, familiar, forgotten feelings' kept walking all over my body. My poor little heart was crying out for him all the time, and just seeing him was all it took for him to capture my whole being. In some way, I was hooked to this man. It could have been because he was the first man to make me love deeply. However, it was evident that the indignity he showed could have made one say forget him, but with me it was different. He was the air I breathed, the food I ate. I loved sex, and he was my fix. Michael was everything wonderful to me. I was afraid, very afraid, because there is always a danger in loving someone so much. When you are not a wife or husband, there is always room for someone else to come and take the other person right from under your nose.

During that week I spent three nights with him. But Michael was busy thinking about his new love Jenny, and when he wrote her a letter and tried to hide it from me, I became suspicious that something was deeply behind it all. It just wasn't a letter, so when he went to the bath-room, I took it from his bag and put it under the micro-wave in the kitchen.

I watched him go through his bag with a puzzled look on his face, and then a shy smile came to his lips as he fixed his eyes on me. My look dared him to ask me about it, but he didn't. After he left for work, I tore the letter to pieces without reading its contents. I knew my poor little heart could not take the blow if I read that Michael was professing his love for someone else. I told myself that what I thought, and what was the actual truth had no bearing on each other.

Michael told me that I could not see him that night, as he was having a visitor. I knew before he went any fur-ther with his explanation that it was Jenny. I could not fathom the notion that he could really invite her to my town. After all, this was my turf. How dare he?

That night when Jenny arrived in town, it was the be-ginning of a trial of fate. It caused a mixed reaction from my friends and especially among Sandra and her friends. Jenny was the woman whom Michael would leave me for. She was the woman who later told me that she wasn't going to leave Michael and that I should "go away qui-etly." Looking back now, neither Sandra nor Jenny could compete with me on any level. I was gorgeous, educated, and had a bubbling personality and a wicked sense of humor. Michael could not believe I could really fall for him and always felt intimidated by my accomplishments. He was never 100% comfortable with me being me. He was also afraid of my father and knew he never approved of Michael as my boyfriend. Michael seemed to be more comfortable in the company of other women. He might have disclosed this to Jean, but all during the time we were together, he never told me of his misgivings.

So when Michael and Jenny went to the nearby club, Sandra whispered a prayer to God, a prayer of thanks that the relationship between Michael and me had, at long last, ended.

The next day I went shopping, and it was there that I was greeted with some mocking remarks from Sandra and her friends. I couldn't stop them; if I had made myself into a fool for love, then let them mock me further. I was humiliated, though, and I knew I had to do something, and I had to do it fast.

I went home and packed a bag with some of my clothing. Where I was going I didn't know, but I had to get away from the laughter. I couldn't stay and face the entire town laughing at me, as they had done to my mom. I waited for Michael, and when he came home, he gave me a big hug, though my body was lifeless in response.

"I missed you last night, Mandy," he began. "I just wanted to be by myself last night."

"Well, you got your wish," I replied.

"Yeah, listen, Mandy, sometimes things are not what they seem to be. I had to straighten something out, but I took care of it.

"I really don't want you to listen to your friends and upset yourself over this; you are my woman, and no one can come between us."

He held me closer to him, and I could hear the rhythm of his heart beating against my face.

"Come home with me for the weekend."

"I can't leave tonight," I said. "But I will come tomorrow afternoon."

I didn't mention the girls and their remarks to him. Instead, I pretended everything was all right.

An hour after Michael left, I took my bag and rushed out the door. I got into my car and pulled out the driveway. Jean was pulling in; we hardly spoke these days after I came back from the States and went right back to Michael; almost everyone just let me be. She didn't know that I was running away—running away from the laughter, running away from the shame, running away from what I myself had helped create. All the pain and the hurt were like a big bountiful harvest I was now reaping.

"I see you are going away for the weekend," she said.

"Yes, and maybe longer."

"What happened? Why are you so sad? Where is Michael?"

"He left already."

"Mandy, you are shaking. You should calm down before you go on the road."

"No, I will be fine," I assured her.

I felt a stab of pain deep within as everything came over me. I felt my head spinning; I tried to think clearly, but to me it was like a big group of lions were coming after me, and I was running as fast as I could before they could devour my body. I wanted to be alone—alone so that when I cried no one would hear and no one would turn their pitiful eyes upon me and offer words of comfort.

Where was I going to be alone? Who could help me find that place? How long would I be able to run for? And how could I survive for the period? The strong would be able to, but I was weak.

My eyes were burning, my heart was aching, and my pride was dying.

Where I was going to spend the night wasn't my problem; it was the thought of eliminating me from society that I quickly dismissed from my mind.

My head was still hurting, and my heart was broken to pieces. I needed solace.

Where the hell was I going?

Where?

Where?

Chapter Ten

It was 7:45 p.m. when I arrived at Cross Road in Kingston. The streets were crowded with people going to the movies at the nearby cinemas. I slowly drove along, thinking maybe I should just go see a movie, check into a hotel, and call it a night.

I was like a frightened child running away from home; therefore, I had to keep on running. I made a U-turn at the light and turned on Slipe Pen Road.

At 7:56 p.m. I was at the front desk asking the operator to put a call through to the host on one of the radio programs. She told me I had to wait for the news break.

At 8:01 p.m. I was talking to the operator again, who was now telling me that Mr. Goulbourne would be coming down to see me. I waited in silence.

As I watched my brother as he came toward me, I observed that he looked the same even though I hadn't seen him in almost a year. Nothing had changed about him.

He greeted me with a smile and a hug. I was glad that I had the chance to tell him that I was on the run. Yes, I was running away from the people, running away from the talk. I just wanted to be alone to sort myself out; after all, it felt like I was losing my sanity.

"Are you sure you are doing the right thing?" he asked.

"I really don't know. I am confused. Please find me a place to stay where I'll be alone and no one will ever find me," I stated.

"Mandy, tell me exactly what happened."

"I will tell you, maybe tomorrow, but not tonight. Tonight I want to get away from it all. Are you going to help me?" I pleaded.

"I'll do anything to help you," he said.

It was 11:00 p.m. when we drove up to the gate and stopped. The house was in the Cherry Gardens Area on the hills of St. Andrew. He took my bag and led the way. The house was a very large colonial-style one. Bombay mango trees lined the front lawn.

He opened the door, and we went inside. The entire place was silent. I wondered if we were alone as I looked around the house. I sat in the large living room while he went to the kitchen to make tea. On his return he told me that it was his aunt's residence and that she lived there with her husband and their two daughters.

His wife, the young and lovely Kandi, was in the United State studying. So, most of the time he stayed with his aunt. "They know you are here and will be coming down to meet you."

"Oh no. Do they know I am your half-sister?"

"Yes, they know you are my rich sister," He smiled at me.

I sat there drinking the tea he had made when two young ladies hurried down the stairs followed by an elderly woman, who I later called, "Aunt Suzie." One of the young ladies looked at me and smiled and introduced herself as Nancy, and the other one as Beth. I was shown to one of the guest rooms beside Nancy's. I took a bath and then joined Paul in the living room.

"Are you OK?" he asked, a concerned look on his face.

"Yes, I think so," I replied.

But I wasn't. I wanted to be by myself and not in the company of these people.

I felt like screaming my head off or getting up and running through the darkness of the night.

Yet I stayed. That night I cried myself to sleep.
This was my exile.

Chapter Eleven

Saturday

I woke up at 8:05 a.m. I looked around the room; it was very comfortable. I opened the window, and the warm glow of sunlight reflected on my skin. The phone rang:

"Hello."

"Hello, Mandy, are you OK?"

"Yes," I replied.

"May I send up something for you to eat?"

"Yes."

Ten minutes later, there was a knock on the door. I opened it to see Nancy standing there with a tray. I took the tray from her, thanking her, and placed it on the bedside table. I didn't want anything to eat. I tried to figure out if my mind was clearing a bit. This was the first day for me in my so-called exile.

I sat by the open window, and slowly, everything was coming back to me. It was four years ago on a bright and sunny day like this that I had first met Michael.

Michael was so unique that I had put him in a class of his own. I had everything as a child, and when my parents divorced, my dad made sure that I still had everything I needed. I had had a good upbringing, so how could I have ended up with a man who was not willing to be with me 100%? I couldn't see that other guys wanted to be with me; I was very popular with a bubbling personality, and I was well-liked. I was fun to be around. So why was I settling for Michael and the baggage that came with him? He already had two kids with Sandra and God knows who else. Why was I letting him bring me to this low point in my life that I felt the need to be hidden away from everyone?

Here I was in a strange house with people I didn't know, except for my brother, wallowing in my grief over Michael; these were his family members, not mine. My thoughts were broken by the ring of the telephone.

"Hello."

"Hello, Mandy. I am coming up to see you."

"OK, that's fine with me."

I hung up the phone and looked around the room; the bed wasn't made, I hadn't eaten, and I was still in my sleepwear. I heard footsteps outside followed by a knock on the door. I turned the lock and opened the door, and there stood Paul.

He stepped inside and closed the door. I watched as his eyes moved around the room.

He looked at the tray and then at me.

"I see you haven't eaten."

"I don't feel like eating anything right now," I told him.

"Mandy, you should have your meals, at least two per day. Please try to understand that," he stated.

"Paul, right now there are things far more important that I want to understand and wish I could understand, but my mind won't let me."

"Maybe I can help you understand; I want to help you, if only you will let me," he stated.

"No, I have told myself so many times, no! No one will ever be able to understand," I told him. "I'd rather you leave now."

"OK, I'll leave, but I will call you later from work to check on you."

I didn't answer him. I watched him as he walked to-ward the door.

Paul might be able to understand; after all, he knew all my problems with Michael. In fact, he did warn me years ago that Michael was not the settling-down type. Why hadn't I stopped the relationship before it reached this stinging climax?

That afternoon I didn't have dinner with the family; instead, I went downstairs and got a glass of milk and came back to my room. I was so embarrassed and ashamed for the way I used to threaten my brother, and here I was now, him becoming my saving grace. If only we had been close growing up, then I wouldn't feel so all alone and could confide in him more. Maybe if I had told him about me being raped he would have seen to it that I got counseling. Earlier when I thought of telling him, I just let it go.

The phone rang, but I just sat there staring at it. At 5:30 p.m. the phone rang again, and I walked to the window and gazed at the empty streets. I heard the door open and turned around to see Paul and Nancy standing there.

"You're looking much better. Do you want to go for a ride?" Paul asked.

"No," I replied.

Nancy gave me the parcel she had in her hands. "This is for you. I hope you like it," she said.

"Thanks, but you didn't have to do this," I said. "Allowing me to stay in your home is already so generous."

I opened the gift box and stared at the lovely gown, but before I could say anything Paul said, "I am taking you to the Press Association Ball, which will be held at the Hilton Hotel."

I looked at him and then at Nancy.

"Thanks to both of you, but I don't wish to go."

"Excuse us for a minute, Nancy," Paul stated.

I watched as she unlocked the door and stepped outside.

"Mandy, you can't do this to us," Paul protested. "Nancy spent a lot of time trying to find you that dress; we all thought you would love it."

"I didn't say I didn't love the dress; I said I didn't want to go to the ball," I said, trying to get my point across.

"Everyone here will be going; I don't want to leave you here by yourself, and I want to introduce you to my coworker Jerry McBright."

I knew Jerry McBright. I did a project in college and had to interview him; however, I'm sure he didn't know I was Paul's sister then.

Jerry McBright was a distinguished journalist who had received many prestigious awards in his field. He was also working part-time as a moderator for a program called, *Jamaica Now* "I have met Jerry already," I told Paul. "He is hot, but I'm not impressed." I smiled at the memory.

"Mandy, just come. You will have a good time."

"OK, fine." I finally said, giving in.

At the Press Association Ball, everyone looked great. The music was good, and everyone was dancing and having a good time. The presentations were made to distinguished journalists who earned special awards. The guest speaker gave his address and urged the journalists to continue their good work of bringing the news of the day to the public. The band started playing again, and most people took to the floor with their special someone.

"Do you care to dance, Mandy?" Paul asked.

"No, not really."

"I miss my wife," he said. "I don't know how I've gotten through these months without her. I can't wait for her to come home next month ".

I could hear the raw sadness in his voice as he looked across the dance floor.

McBright came over and held my hand, so I went to dance with him for a while as he quizzed me like I was part of the local news. I wasn't in the mood for all of his questions, but I remembered how nice he was to me that day years ago, even having taken me to lunch. The music stopped, and we headed to the bar. I ordered tonic water while he had scotch.

"I saw your father earlier today with his family at the mall," he said. "I asked about you, and he said you are about to get married." McBright looked at me with a puzzled look on his face. "Are you still with your deadbeat boyfriend?"

"No." I held up my hand to show him there was no ring on my finger. A wide smile came across his face as he brought my hand to his lips.

"Let's date. I want to marry you," he said.

I couldn't help myself, but I burst out laughing. I laughed so much my head began to hurt.

"I told you this three years ago, remember? We had a one-night stand and I wanted to be with you, and you said, 'Just pretend this never happened,'" he said with such conviction in his voice as he pulled me closer to him.

"No," I said softly, "I don't remember." I walked over to my brother.

"Are you ready to leave?" he asked.

"Honestly, Paul, yes. I wish I could stay longer, but my head hurts."

McBright quickly walked over to us. "Are you guys leaving?" he asked.

"Yes," Paul said. "Mandy isn't feeling well, so I am taking her home."

"I will take her home; I need to talk to her on the way," McBright told him.

"No, Jerry, I will take my sister home, end of discussion. Let's go," he said as he ushered me away from McBright and to the door.

As Paul, Nancy, and I left the hotel, it was almost 2:00 a.m. Once we got back to the house, I went to bed and somehow fell asleep.

What the breaking of day held I didn't know.

Chapter Twelve

Sunday

That Sunday morning I woke up crying. I must have cried for a long time. It was 9:00 a.m. when the phone rang.

I picked it up and uttered, "Yes?"

"Are you ready for breakfast?"

"Y...yes." I struggled to get the word out.

I turned on the radio and heard one of those religious programs.

I listened to the choir as they sang out with their voices the familiar song, "Just as I Am."

Just as I am, without one plea
but that thy blood was shed for me,

and that thou bidst me come to thee,
O Lamb of God, I come, I come.

I remembered that it was that same song that had led me to the altar on my knees four years ago. I remembered giving my life to God that night and further taking my step with Him through the waters of baptism. What had led me away from that church or from the cross where I first saw the light was now haunting me as the music continued.

Just as I am, thy love unknown
hath broken every barrier down;
now, to be thine, yea thine alone,
O Lamb of God, I come...

There was a knock on the door.

"Come in," I called.

Paul and Nancy walked in with my breakfast. Nancy placed the tray on the bedside table and left.

My head was turned to the wall, and tears were running down my cheeks while I sobbed loudly.

Paul walked over and put his arms around me.

"Mandy, please don't cry," he said as he tried to comfort me.

But I just couldn't hold back my tears.

"How long have you been crying?"

I didn't answer. He sat beside me for several minutes, and neither of us spoke.

He took a glass with orange juice from the tray and brought it to my lips. I tasted it and put it away. I tried to calm down, but the more I realized that it was Sunday, the more upset I got. I looked through the window and saw people going to church; I saw the little children going to Sunday school, and it certainly brought back memories.

I had grown up attending Sunday school, but something out there was haunting me—something that gave me no peace of mind or urges to go back to the fellowship of the church. I remembered saying a prayer to God. My heart was beating fast, and I could feel the pain as it pierced through my flesh.

A flesh of corruption.

Paul left and I fell asleep.

At noon I got out of bed, showered, got dressed, and went downstairs with the breakfast tray. I could see the worried look on Aunt Suzie's face as she noticed that the food was untouched.

"Mandy, you must try and eat something; this is not good for you."

"Please, Aunt Suzie. Don't worry about me; I will be all right."

"You can't be if you are not eating," she scolded.

"I know but…but it's just that…that…"

"Just what, Mandy?" she asked as she patted me on my shoulders.

"You will never understand, Aunt Suzie; you will never understand."

"Let's talk about it, Mandy. Don't be afraid; you can trust me."

"Thanks, Aunt Suzie, but I am not ready to talk about it."

As the day continued, it was a rather quiet Sunday, the very first one I could recall in a very long time. I tried to tell myself that I would be going home tomorrow, that I was only spending a weekend.

I must be strong, I must go back and face it all, I thought, and then those thoughts flashed out of my mind.

I spent the rest of the afternoon with Nancy. At 11:00 p.m., I went to bed praying for peace of mind.

Monday

Monday morning at 5:00 a.m., I awoke depressed. I wasn't working, and I kept thinking about my past jobs.

How could I possibly be losing out when I had so many opportunities?

My life had already been paved for me; all I had to do was make the right decisions and follow the path. However, so far all I had done was make decisions that were wrong, and I continued to head down a path of self-destruction. Here I was in a stranger's house hiding away from society when, indeed, society had been very good to me. My eyes were burning, and I went back to sleep.

Later, I went downstairs for the first time to have breakfast with the family.

"Good morning, Mandy. You are looking lovely this morning," remarked Aunt Suzie.

"Thank you. I feel lovely too," I replied.

"I'm glad you decided to join us."

We all sat at the table, and for the first time since I had arrived there, I felt like I was indeed a part of this beautiful family and not intruding on them.

She might have been reading my mind when she said, "Paul speaks very highly of you, and I want you to know that we are happy to have you."

"Thank you."

I spent the rest of the day with her. We talked about teenage pregnancies and politics, but we never ventured into the area of relationships. An experienced woman like Aunt Suzie knew I wasn't ready to awake those demons and pour out my soul to her.

That evening Paul told me that he would play a "special selection" for me on his radio program. He went on further to say that he was prepared to stay up with me that night and let me pour out my soul.

I went to my room and tried to relax. I turned on the radio and listened to a part of the radio show; sure enough I heard the selection being dedicated to me—Roger Whittaker's "The Last Farewell." Such a beautiful song. I then turned off the radio. Was it that I was saying the last farewell to love? After this would I be able to love again?

Paul came up to my room later that night.

"Did you enjoy the selection?" he asked.

"I didn't listen," I lied.

"It was 'The Last Farewell.' You should have listened."

"I must have dozed off," I replied.

"Let's talk," he said.

I told him everything. The words didn't come as freely as I had thought they would. There were times when I had difficulties in expressing some episodes. I broke down three times while relaying the story to him.

He listened and didn't ask many questions. Paul, more than anyone, was familiar with Michael's womanizing and had warned me about him in the earlier days. Tonight he said to me, "Michael knows you are one woman who will never leave him—you will always be there—and so he will continue to play the field. However, I believe Michael loves you but just not enough to settle down."

When will I get that in my thick head?

"You are my sister, and I have told you on more than one occasion to cut him loose. He has issues he never dealt with, and he is only going to please himself. I think why you two fit so well is because he lost the only person he ever loved in a tragic way and you lost your family due to Dad's behavior. You grew up feeling unloved. Having said this, I will say I have always loved you, and I never held it against you for the way I was treated by your mom."

"Have you forgiven me for the way I always cursed you out?" I whispered.

"A long time ago, we were never responsible for our upbringing; we were kids," he said. "I have to ask you this—why did you came back from America? It was your only chance of getting rid of Michael, but you came right back to him. Can you understand why your friends shun you? Can you understand why Dad has given up on you?"

Without waiting for me to answer, he walked toward the door and turned off the lights.

I was so relieved knowing I had, indeed, poured my soul out to someone who understood—someone who could see that I had loved beyond reason.

Tuesday

It was a bright day; the sunlight flowed through the open window in my room. I heard the sound of a police car hurry by; it was about noon. Unknown to me, my dear father had learned of my strange disappearance and was worried about me. He drove over ninety miles to get information from my close friends whom he thought would lead him to my whereabouts.

Meanwhile, Paul and I were having a chat in my room.

"Are you feeling better?"

"Much better," I replied.

"Mandy, after I saw you break down last night while relating those episodes, I realized how love can destroy one's self when used in a destructive manner. You have to know where to draw the line; I learned something from you last night."

"Paul, I want to be strong. It has been strength and courage that have helped me go on, but now it seems I have lost. I have paid the price, and I need to feel sorry for myself."

"Mandy, I feel for you, I really do. I'm glad you came to me; you know I could never let you down," he said.

"I know. You have been so good to me."

We went down for dinner, and afterward he left for work. That night I heard the song "The Greatest Love" by George Benson from Muhammad Ali's motion picture *The Greatest*.

I cried myself to sleep.

Wednesday

With the heat of the morning penetrating through my body, I sat down peacefully and wrote the following letter:

My Dear Jean,

Let me hope you are not worrying too much about me; I am all right. You ought to believe that.

My behavior last Friday was very strange, but some-day it will be revealed to you and to others.

I had to leave last Friday. When I return home, I will be a different person. The changes are already taking place. Let me assure you that I love you as a friend, but there comes a time when one has to sort out his or her own problems. With God's help, I am getting through.

I need your prayers.

Mandy

Chapter Thirteen

The fear of what might have happened to me or what I might have done to myself was taking a toll on my friends and family. Michael had become a public enemy to all my friends but was trying to convince everyone who would listen that "things were good between us."

He told my dad that I was supposed to be with him that weekend but that I hadn't shown up; he said that when he left the previous evening, we had parted on good terms, so there was nothing amiss. When my dad asked him about the woman who came to visit him in my town, he said there was no woman and that it was just a rumor started by Sandra and her friends and that he would not have done that to me; even to this day Michael would still swear that meeting never happened.

So even when he called Paul, pouring out his frustrations about my behavior, Paul pretended to be deeply concerned but told him he had not heard from me.

However, when my dad came looking for me, Paul had no option but to tell him the truth.

Thursday

I opened the window like I did each morning and looked over the hills of St. Andrew. I saw the beautiful scenery of the city below. It was like a paradox that perplexed my soul. Why didn't I just go into the city and find Michael? He must have been worried to death about me. About that time, a car pulled up, and my father got out. He looked up and saw me by the window, and I waved to him.

I went downstairs to meet my dad, and we embraced warmly.

Upstairs in my room, my father was furious with me and let me know in no uncertain terms.

"I know I might not be a good example for you, so you won't listen to me, but it's time for you to forget Michael and move on with your life," he said. "I told you before and I am telling you now: he is bad news; leave him while you still can."

I looked at my dad, and his words pierced my heart as he continued.

"You love him too much, and he doesn't love you enough; he is selfish and will continue to do whatever pleases him. Let go, Mandy. Please let go. I don't want to lose you."

"You won't," I assured him.

"Mandy, I want you to promise me you won't go back to Michael."

"I can't, Dad; I am trying to promise myself first."

"Your mother filed for you, you have US residency, yet you don't want to live there. Four months was not enough time for you to adjust. Do you want to go back? Or maybe you could go to London or Canada," he said.

"Why, Dad?" I asked.

"Why? I am trying to save my daughter, that's why."

"I will be just fine," I told my father.

I then watched as he left my room and then walked to his car and drove away.

I took a nap and was later awakened by a knock on my door. Nancy stood there.

"Your dad is on the phone," she said.

I took the phone from her and listened to my father screaming in my ears.

I placed the phone down and began packing my things. My dad said he would be there within the hour to get me. I went to find Paul.

"Dad wants me to go home," I told him.

"Yeah, I know," he said.

I looked at Paul with a puzzled look on my face.

"Did he tell you he spent all afternoon looking for Michael after he left here?"

"No, why was he looking for him?"

"To tell him to stay away from you."

"He did *what*?"

"You heard me; however, I told Dad that his problem is not with Michael; it is with you. Mandy, I am telling you again to push Michael to the curb and be the woman you are capable of being. Love will find you again, but if you destroy yourself now, you will never be able to experience true love."

I hugged my brother and thanked him for being there for me.

"Mandy, I am going to miss you, but I am always a phone call away, and I will be in touch."

"You certainly will. I have decided to move in the house at Sharrow Drive," I told him.

"Wonderful. When?" he asked.

"As soon as Dad can arrange for the workmen to do the necessary renovations—about a week or two from now."

"Michael will want to come and live with you," he stated.

"Michael, why?"

"Well, I still think you two are going to patch things up."

"Paul, if you were in my position, what would you do?" I asked.

"I would have ended the relationship long ago. What has made you hold on for so long?"

"I really don't know, Paul, but this time it just has to be over, even though I have said that time after time."

"Mandy, don't worry. Things will work out for you pretty soon, and if they don't, McBright is waiting in the wings," he said, smiling.

"What do you know about that?"

"Nothing, but he is crazy about you."

He smiled at me then continued. "Call me when you get home."

"Thanks again, Paul."

I went to kiss Aunt Suzie and Nancy.

I sat with my dad enjoying the ride even though it was mostly in silence.

When I arrived home, Jean and I hugged. It was like the return of the prodigal son; my exile had ended.

Chapter Fourteen

Two days later, I saw Michael, and we had a long talk. I told him everything about my soul-searching six days. He was very upset. He sincerely promised me that he was going to change, that he wasn't going to hurt me anymore, but I knew those were mere empty words.

Could my heart take any more of this crazy man's behavior?

"Let's talk, Mandy. It's us against everyone else." He was staring at me so hard I felt uncomfortable.

"No one loves you—your mom left you to fend for yourself, and your father thinks giving you material things is all it takes to raise a child. The brother you grew up hating doesn't care about you, so right now I am the only one—yes, the only one—who really loves you," he stated defiantly.

"I am losing my family because of you," I told him.

"You have no family!" he shouted.

I stood there, hot tears running down my cheeks. Between my tears I could see him with a look of satisfaction on his face.

He walked over to me and wiped the tears from my eyes and put his arms around me

"How dare they? Which one of your family members ever tried to get you help? Which one of them?" he asked.

"When my father died, he was my world, and my family knew that, so they all rallied around me and showed me love and care. I rejected their intervention to help because I wanted to do it on my own. I had that choice; you didn't." He continued, "They think you are too good for me because I am nothing in their eyes."

I moved toward the table and sat on the edge. I felt faint as his words hit me.

"My past was always the path to my survival. I didn't want to end up like my mother, but I was like her in so many ways. I am still hurting from the rape, which I haven't been able to tell anyone about, and I have lost all my friends, just like my mother did years ago. Even though my brother has forgiven me, I still remember when I was living with Julie that I blamed him and his mom for destroying my mother. Every time we had an argument, I would scream at him, 'Your mother is a whore! Your mother is a whore!' And he would just look at me and shake his head. I regret every moment of those temper tantrums."

Michael was right. I always isolated myself and spent a lot of time in my room—time that could have been better spent with my brother. I looked at Michael; I had never been talked down to like this before, and every word he said resonated with who I was and somehow contrasted with who I was trying to be. My heart was bursting with shame, guilt, and most of all, the loneliness that was always me.

"So what gives them the right to think that you are better than I am? You're not better, Mandy; we are equal in every way."

"Fuck you, Michael! Fuck you!"

"Yeah, that's what we are going to do to each other," he said, a smirk on his face as he stared at me.

I went in my room and locked the door. I stood with my back bracing the door as if he was coming after me, but all was quiet. I stumbled onto the bed like a drunken sailor. I woke up in the wee hours, went to the kitchen to get a glass of milk, and Michael was nowhere to be seen. He must have left, I thought. However, when I returned to my room, he was in my bed.

I knew then that true love never dies and people never stop loving someone who they really love. There was no way I could ever stop loving Michael. However, so many people couldn't be wrong; we looked good together, but we were clearly wrong for each other. My father was so frustrated and worried about my emotional state that he would do anything just to get me away from Michael.

So from then on, I knew I would have to live with my feelings for Michael wrapped up within me, and sure enough, that night I made up my mind to walk out of Michael's life and say good-bye to a lover I could not possibly forget. The pain of holding onto him versus the pain of leaving him contrasted one another.

However, tonight, I thought, I would savor the moments.

The next morning when I awoke and went to the kitchen, Michael was preparing breakfast; he kissed me on the cheek as I walked in.

"Hi. Breakfast is ready."

"I'm not hungry, but I will have coffee."

"Only coffee? You didn't really eat all day yesterday," he reminded me.

"Yes, I know but—"

"But what?" he paused. "Believe me, Mandy. Everything is going to be just fine, just the two of us," he said, putting his arms around me. I moved away and poured myself some coffee.

"Want coffee?" I asked.

"No, tea," he said.

He joined me at the table a minute later.

"Look, Mandy, I know it's hard on you. I have put you through hell, but believe me, I swear I'll never hurt you again," he said.

I looked at him and sighed.

"Michael, it's no use. I have reached the end of my rope, and I can't take anymore. Can't you see what you have done to me?"

My hands shook so badly that my coffee cup fell to the floor and broke into pieces.

"Calm down, Mandy," he said.

"How many more lies must I listen to? How many more promises? How many more pleas? You tell me, how many more?" I screamed at him.

"OK, calm down. What do you want, Mandy?" he asked.

"I just want you out of my life so that I can pick up the pieces while I'm still able to do so."

"We have come a long way. I can't let you go now," he said.

"Michael, I have made up my mind; it's over," I said sadly.

"No, Mandy, we have only just begun."

"Michael, please don't break me anymore. I can't go on like this; please don't do this to me. Can't you see I've almost lost my sanity?"

He held me close, caressing my hair. I could hear the beating of his heart against my ears, and for that moment I thought he was my all.

"Mandy, I can't leave you this way."

"I'll be fine; I don't need your pity."

"Are you going to miss me?" he asked teasingly.

"Sure, I will miss you."

"Then I won't leave you, Mandy. I swear to God I won't," he said.

"No, just go!" I sobbed. "We have no life together; make it easy on me and go now," I pleaded.

I watched him as he stared at me; his eyes were watery, but his face betrayed nothing, no visible sign of remorse or reminiscence of happier times. We sat there for a long time, and neither of us spoke.

"I am moving in today," he said calmly.

"Where?" I asked, shocked.

"Here. I am coming to live with you, and maybe we can get married later in the year."

"Are you sure that's what you really want?"

"Yes, I love you, and I want to be with you always."

Michael moved in. We were going to make it this time; I just knew it. We were not going to hurt each other again. However, it was only ten months later that he hurt me more than I could ever live to forgive him.

Chapter Fifteen

The months were long and hard, and I suffered secretly more than anyone could imagine.

Those months were trying ones, and neither of us wanted to let go. There were times when we were together and it was magical, and then there were always the moments I dreaded—the reality that he might not come home, I thought I would feel better now that we are living together; however, my state of mind got worse. It was not until he arrived home each evening that my fears were driven away and I could be thankful. My Dad had not spoken to me in over ten months and my brother was so upset with me, and that just added to my day to day worries.

I sat in Dr. Jones's office with a placid look on my face, not wanting my emotions to betray the joy I was feeling.

"Mandy, your test is positive. You are eight weeks pregnant."

A shy smile crept over my lips.

"Aren't you happy?" he asked.

Happy? I questioned myself.

"Yes, doctor, I am very happy," I replied.

I walked out the doctor's office to my car. Upon reaching home, I called Michael and told him the news; his voice betrayed no emotion. My heart sank as I hung up the phone. I went to my room and locked myself in. Something was totally wrong; I could feel it. Michael had not shared the joy I felt.

I tried to reason it away, but it kept coming back.

That evening, when Michael came home, he told me I should have an abortion. It was useless arguing with him. However, I had long ago made up my mind to have my baby, and no one was going to change that. So with all the time I had before the baby would be born, I made up my mind to deal my own cards; I wasn't going to play with a stacked deck for anyone. It seemed this was going to drive him away. He didn't want to have a child. He said no more children for him right now; I honestly had no idea how many children he really had out there running around. I firmly said no abortion, not this time; the first one I had was out of shame. I told him that I would raise this child and try to do a good job at it. However, I wanted to say, "Please stay. I am not strong enough for the anguish of you leaving." But I didn't.

I listened to his footsteps coming through the front door. I sat there searching, but what more was there to find? I was a lost cause to my family. Most of my friends basically just stayed away from me. I felt Michael in every inch of me—even more as I was carrying his child. I could never stop loving him, and even when the impossible proved me wrong, I had always given in. For Michael to leave me, that would have been the final blow; however, I could not use my present state to stop him from going.

Two days later, he was gone. I cried myself to sleep like I had done so many nights before.

I was weak; I had no courage to go on. I woke up crying. No matter how hard I tried, the memories held me, trying so hard not to let me go. I knew I couldn't possibly forget the deeply felt emotions of the past that drew me to ecstasy in his world. The sweet lovemaking—oh, the sex between us was glorious. I could feel it in my soul; it was a feeling like nothing else mattered when we were together between the sheets. When we made love, I could feel my heart, my body, and my soul entwined with his. I know he felt it too, as many times after we made love he would run his hand through my hair and place kisses on my face, while other times he would hold me in his arms so tightly that I could hear the rhythm of his heartbeat. Without this man I was doomed. My father's words rang true again.

I gazed out the window, and the truth stood out and touched every bone in me—the truth that this child that I was carrying might never share a bond with his father. The hurt was building up inside of me, and I knew then the birth of this child was going to change my life completely. I tried hopelessly to control myself under the conditions. I couldn't survive; under this condition I just couldn't make it.

Two weeks later, I heard Michael had left the island. I remembered someone once said, "Loneliness is never more cruel than when it is felt in close proximity with someone who has ceased to communicate." I sat there for hours with a battered heart and tears rolling down my cheeks like a small child. Why was Michael destroying me like this?

The answer stared me in the face. Yes, everything he had done to me was justified, and he knew it because I had allowed him to play with my emotions. If he had stood by me now, he would have done so out of pity, just as he had done before. I was convinced that we were two lost souls trying to find our way in life and ended up with each other repeatedly. I realized then how delirious I was to even harbor such thoughts. However, this time I was given justice in the name of love.

Chapter Sixteen

I was in my ninth month, and each time the baby leapt in my womb, it brought me closer to the responsibility of becoming a mother. My world was full of disappointments, bitter memories, and heartaches. My world was no place for a child. I was at the entrance of a mental institution, begging to go in; even if I held out a little longer, what could I do for this child? It was a total shame how Michael had deserted me; I could not do that to my baby. I had already accepted my fate; as a mother I could not disown my child or run away from my duties.

It was 10:15 a.m. Monday morning, and the nurse held the baby for me to see, and then I heard the first cry.

After thirty-four hours of labor, it was finally over. The ordeal was very bittersweet. If it hadn't been for the hardworking team of professionals, Aiden's birth might not have been a reality.

I spent three days in the hospital. Jean came to see me daily, and Paul was there to give me the moral support I needed. I watched Paul hold Aiden for the first time, and I couldn't help wondering if Aiden would ever know his own father's touch. Having and caring for Aiden had given me more strength and determination to make my life worth living again.

Three months had passed, and early one morning I had just gotten back from taking Aiden for a walk, and I was sitting on the back porch feeding him when I heard a car coming up the driveway. I went to see who was paying us a visit this early. I stopped dead in my tracks when I saw Michael ascending the steps to the front door. It had been almost eight months since I had last seen him. Was I really ready to face him?

I knew one day he would be back. I had never given up on his return, and then there he was. He stopped in the doorway as he saw the baby in my arms.

"Hi," he said, coming closer. He stretched out his hands for Aiden, but I held the baby closer.

He stepped back, a worried look on his face.

"I'm home, Mandy. Here is where I belong with you and my..." He paused.

142

Then I realized he didn't know, and from somewhere inside me those wounds burst and tears started flowing so raw like tears of blood. He took the baby from me eagerly.

"It's a boy," I said.

Then suddenly I noticed the wedding band on his finger. I stood there motionless; an attack of nausea took hold of me, and my body started shaking, and the place began to spin around me as darkness overshadowed and plunged me into a bottomless pit.

The color of the room came slowly as I focused my eyes on the wall. It wasn't familiar at first.

I lay still, trying to gain my memory; everything was blank. I stared at the ceiling then the floor, yet there was nothing, no similarities.

I looked at the walls all around, and from somewhere inside me the laughter came like a cry at first, then louder and louder into a state of hysterical melody echoing in the hallways.

The door opened, and a lady dressed in white held my hands.

"Let me go! Take your filthy hands off me! Let me go, you dirty bitch!" I screamed. Then I felt the needle in my hand, and I was once again in the darkness that gave me peace of mind.

I had lost track of time and had lost everything; I didn't wish to know who I was anymore. I opened my eyes to the ceiling once again, then for the first time I realized I was wearing clothes. I began tearing them off piece by piece until I was the way God had made me. All those clothes were covering my sins, and I wanted to purify myself. Bit by bit, I dropped the raiment on the floor.

Suddenly, I stopped; something was coming. Slowly, I tried to think again

"Lover of my...child, child?"

I repeated over and over.

"My child, lover of my child."

Then I remembered.

My baby Aiden! I wanted my baby!

And then came the pain of the needle again and a man caressing my face while the lady in white covered me with a large white blanket.

My nakedness meant nothing to them; they had seen so many before in my state.

To them I was just another who had lost sanity.

I was later removed from the hospital and placed in a private facility where I spent almost two months. The recuperation period wasn't easy, but I was able to pull through. Michael was indeed married.

My breakdown had really shaken him up, and he had made a decision to end his marriage and remain with us. However, the pain was too much for me; just seeing him in the house was more than I could handle.

Four months after, Michael changed his job. All the sacrifices he was now making were "too little, too late."

Nothing could ever be the same again, because I had paid the price.

Chapter Seventeen

Two months later, Michael moved out—this time for good. I couldn't stand to see him in the house one more day. We were living together in the same house, but I didn't talk to him; we slept in separate rooms. I even avoided going to the kitchen if I knew he was there. I ceased from answering the phone; I had lost all feeling to communicate. So there I was living in total isolation.

However, that morning before he left he came to my room.

"Good-bye, Mandy," he said.

"Bye," I said.

"I have one last request," he stated.

"What is it?" I asked.

"I want to see my son, so please arrange for me to see him," he pleaded.

"Aiden doesn't need you. Just get out!" I shouted.

I heard the door slam, and then the car drove away. I listened as it roared in the distance until I could hear it no more. How long I sat there I didn't know. The phone kept on ringing, and I didn't even hear it. The echoing sound of Michael's car was still real to me until I heard the doorbell ringing and the pounding sound on the door.

"Mandy, open the door. I know you are in there. It's Paul."

His voice seemed like it was a thousand miles away, and then the distance came simultaneously with the reality of the present.

"Mandy, open the door!"

I went downstairs, and as I looked through the glass door, I saw two police cars parked outside.

I reluctantly opened the door. When I saw the pained look on Paul's face, I knew something tragic had happened.

"It's Aiden, isn't it?" I asked.

"No, it's Michael," he said.

"Michael?" I whispered.

"Yes, he was involved in an accident; he is in the hospital, and he is asking for you," he said.

"When did this happen?" I asked.

"Three hours ago. We have been trying to reach you for the past two hours," he said.

"Will he make it?" I asked, concerned.

"Not sure; he might have lost out by now. We have to hurry," he said.

"Michael was a part of me once, but not anymore; I won't go," I stated.

"Mandy", said Paul, "don't do this, you can't do this now, not when he is dying."

"Call his wife," I stated.

"Michael doesn't have a wife; his marriage was annulled, and you know that!" Paul shot back.

I told Paul that my soul died some time ago, and when it did, Michael died with it also. We don't need each other, neither in life nor in death.

Paul stated that Michael wanted to make peace with me. I told him to let him make peace with his soul and his God.

The phone rang; one of the officers standing nearby went to answer it.

"It's for you, sir," he said, holding the phone out to Paul, and I knew before he even spoke.

"Oh no. No." I watched Paul bury his face in this hand. I rushed over to be at his side.

"That was the hospital; he didn't make it," he said to me, shaking his head in disbelief.

They all left without saying another word to me. I stood in the doorway, yet no tears came.

Deep inside, the reality struck me…I would have to live with this for the rest of my life. I drove him out of the house when he was finally doing everything that he was supposed to do.

He had gone through a great deal to have his marriage annulled. It also cost him a great deal in monetary damages. He said he was ashamed of the way he had treated us and had vowed to be a good father to Aiden and a loving and caring husband to me. Why couldn't I have just let it be and been supportive of him? Instead, I told myself I could never forgive him or forget.

Every inch of my body shook knowing he was now lying in a body bag.

I killed him. If I had put a knife through his heart, I couldn't have done it better.

How was I going to live with myself? The guilt washed over me with such force, like a power hose washing a vehicle. I curled up on the floor and wept. No one was there for me—no friends, no family except for my brother, and you could see the pain mixed with frustration on his face. I hadn't spoken to my father since the day Michael moved in the first time. My dad had written me off. He didn't come to see me at the hospital when I was having the baby. He didn't come to see me when I had my breakdown. I think he just couldn't look at me, and I was spared that pain of seeing my father's anguish. However, I knew I was already dead to him.

The days leading up to the funeral, I was lost and most of the time in a daze. Whenever I ventured out to go food shopping, I thought everyone was talking about me like I was a piece of garbage. The officers had asked during their investigation into the accident about where Michael was going. There were clothes all over the car and in the trunk. I told them we had had a fight and that he was going out to clear his mind. I even stated that we fought all the time and that it was not unusual for him to leave for a while. They didn't believe me. I requested a copy of Michael's cell phone records just to see if he had called anyone on his way from the house that morning, and sure enough, he had called two people: his mother and Paul.

I knew then the secret I had thought I could take to my grave was no longer. They knew I had thrown him out. I was torn to pieces; his mother loved me, and his family loved me, and I killed him. I became sick all over, and then it all started to happen.

The night was still; there seemed to be no stars above. The cool water of the spring flowed gently along its course. It was clear like the reflection of one's self in a mirror, the vivid sight of a lost lover.

The thought of him flashed through my mind. I look around, but he wasn't there.

My whole being reached out for his love, wishing I could touch him, feel his warm body against mine, feel his soft, gentle hands caressing my body.

The night went on, and the memories controlled my mind. I remembered the cries of the mourners at the funeral. I saw his body there void. I wanted to go with him then, but I came to my senses.

He was gone, but I knew Aiden and I must go on living without him.

Suddenly I awoke. The bedside lamp was out, and it was then that I saw the figure coming toward me.

It came closer and closer; a chilly air filled the room, and I saw Michael.

I tried to scream, but no sound came. I lay there still, trying to rid myself of this fear. Why should I be afraid? Michael was dead, and the living and the dead have no dealing. I fell asleep.

Shortly, I was awakened again. This time I saw the figure vaguely smiling and reaching out its hands to touch me. I screamed.

I lay there in the stillness of the night, cold sweat washing over my body and I started crying. When will this nightmare end? When will I be at peace again?

Epilogue

As Mandy finished her recollection of her life with my Son Michael, her words shocked me to the core. I could see she was emotionally spent. She fell asleep and I pulled the blanket over her and closed the bedroom door. I walked towards the window and looked outside; the first light of dawn was breaking through the tall pine trees. I lit a cigarette and exhaled. Her words kept coming back to me and it felt haunting.

I walked to her room and looked in; she was sleeping peacefully. I poured my first cup of coffee and returned to the window with the morning paper. As I was draining the last of my coffee, that's when the deafening sound rang out in the silence of the wee hours like firecrackers—*bang!*

I cradled my daughter-in-law's lifeless body in my arms and wept.

I cried for me.I cried for her mother's poor choice in judgment. Over the years she had lived a rather privileged life in the United States and had no idea that her only child was so troubled.

I cried for Mandy, I cried for my son, Michael, and my Grandson Aiden.

"We will have to take her now."

I carefully laid her on the bed and looked at the faces across the room who had known her, and they all stared back at me like lions waiting on their prey.

I felt the note in my pocket, and then I heard the sound of Aiden crying, and at that moment I knew all was not lost.

The End

About the Author

— **Vern Hamil**

Vern Hamil is a Jamaican born author whose goal is to be renowned in the literary world. She wants her writings to convey a message of hope and inspiration for readers and, in so doing, reach a broad audience.

She has an AS in Business Management and a BS in Business Administration. She is a mother and grandmother and loves to read, write, and cook. She currently resides in Bronx, New York, with her family.

www.ingramcontent.com/pod-product-compliance
Lightning Source LLC
Chambersburg PA
CBHW071130280326
41935CB00010B/1165